THE TRADING FLOORS OF HEAVEN

THE TRADING FLOORS OF HEAVEN

WHERE LOST BLESSINGS ARE RESTORED AND
KINGDOM DESTINY IS FULFILLED

BEVERLEY WATKINS
& ROBERT HENDERSON

© Copyright 2018 – Beverley Watkins and Robert Henderson

All rights reserved. This book is protected by the copyright laws of the United States of America. This book may not be copied or reprinted for commercial gain or profit. The use of short quotations or occasional page copying for personal or group study is permitted and encouraged. Permission will be granted upon request. Unless otherwise identified, Scripture quotations are taken from the New King James Version. Copyright © 1982 by Thomas Nelson, Inc. Used by permission. All rights reserved. Scripture quotations marked AMP are taken from the Amplified® Bible, Copyright © 2015 by The Lockman Foundation, La Habra, CA 90631. All rights reserved. Used by permission. All emphasis within Scripture quotations is the author's own. Please note that Destiny Image's publishing style capitalizes certain pronouns in Scripture that refer to the Father, Son, and Holy Spirit, and may differ from some publishers' styles.

DESTINY IMAGE® PUBLISHERS, INC.
P.O. Box 310, Shippensburg, PA 17257-0310
"Promoting Inspired Lives."

This book and all other Destiny Image and Destiny Image Fiction books are available at Christian bookstores and distributors worldwide.

Cover design by Eileen Rockwell
Interior design by Terry Clifton

For more information on foreign distributors, call 717-532-3040.

Reach us on the Internet: www.destinyimage.com.

ISBN 13 TP: 978-0-7684-1908-5
ISBN 13 eBook: 978-0-7684-1909-2
ISBN 13 HC: 978-0-7684-1911-5
ISBN 13 LP: 978-0-7684-1910-8

For Worldwide Distribution, Printed in the U.S.A.
1 2 3 4 5 6 7 8 / 22 21 20 19 18

Contents

1. The Principle of Spiritual Trading 1
2. Why Is Spiritual Trading Important? 17
3. What Is a Trading Floor? 33
4. Trading in Heaven *by Robert Henderson* 45
5. Trading with the Enemy 57
6. The Greatest Trade of All Time 81
7. It's Time to Recover All 93
8. Trading in the Heavenly Realm 115
9. The Power of Sacrifice 137
10. The Dynamics of Trading *by Robert Henderson* 167
11. Let's Get Trading 183
12. Prayers to Access the Trading Floors of Heaven 193

The Principle of Spiritual Trading

THE FIRST TIME THAT I EVER HEARD THE WORD *trading* used in Christian circles was at a conference. We were in a time of worship and someone on the stage was singing a prophetic song about God's heart for the nations. As they were singing, I saw in the realm of the spirit what looked like a lot of coals lying on the carpet in front of the pulpit. As I stared at the coals, wondering what they were, I heard one of the prophets in the meeting say, "God wants us to come and trade with Him for nations." At the time I had no idea what that meant, but I saw people get up all over the auditorium and start giving money into the offering baskets. I had absolutely no idea what was happening, but my spirit was excited, so I grabbed hold of some money and went and placed it in the offering basket. As I walked toward the basket, I felt extremely hot and sensed such a weight of the presence of God. It was amazing. I knew that something significant had just happened. When I thought about that moment later that day, the idea of trading for nations struck a chord in my spirit. I could not have explained what we were doing to anyone, but I knew it was a God thing!

As I learned more about spiritual trading floors, I quickly realized that finances are only one expression of spiritual trading; they are simply the means through which the Lord introduced me to the concept of the trading floors of Heaven. Perhaps because when it comes to the idea of a "trading floor," what stands out most is the monetary trading that takes place on the New York Stock Exchange.

Over the years, God has slowly taught us more about this "trading." It is not about "doing business" in the church. It is not simply another form of taking an offering or a tithe. It is not a tool to manipulate God. Trading is integral to God's desire to see the Kingdom established on earth as it is in Heaven. It is a function of those who are called to be priests and kings unto our God, so that we can reign on the earth with Him (see Rev. 5:10).

THE ORIGINS OF SPIRITUAL TRADING

The terms *trading* and *trading floor* may be new to you, but the concept of spiritual trading is not a new one. It has been happening in Heaven from the very beginning. Long before the earth was created, before lucifer was removed from Heaven, there was trading in Heaven. Trading and trading floors are not new concepts; they may just be new to this generation of believers who are alive on earth right now!

Trading in the natural is ancient and all encompassing. From the earliest times, people have traded the goods they had to get the goods that they did not have. This early barter trade gave way to mediums of exchange like furs, salt, and weapons before coins were introduced around 600 B.C. This paved the way for the creation of currencies and monetary instruments that we use in our economic system today. Trading (this mutual exchange of goods and services) is the basis of every economy and the way in which all kingdoms expand. Think about it for a moment. Every time you go into a store, you trade for something. You take money that you earned for a service you provided and you exchange that for a loaf of bread—something that you need. In the natural, we all trade all the time. We trade what we have to lay hold of the things that we do not have. It is the foundation of our personal economy. Through trading, we have food to eat, clothes to wear, opportunity to travel, and even access to healthcare and education. Our ability and skill to trade what we have "in our hand" defines our economic success or failure. This applies to us individually, as families, and even as nations. Our ability to trade defines our economy. As in the natural, so it is in the spirit. Our ability to trade in heavenly places with "what is in our hand" will define the spiritual economy that we walk in.

But let's not get ahead of ourselves. Let's begin our journey by going to the place in Scripture where the idea of "trading" as a heavenly activity is first introduced in Ezekiel 28:12-17. The challenge is that if you do not read the verses carefully, you might conclude that the act of "trading" was the reason God removed lucifer from the heavenly realms. So let's take a look at this key Scripture. (The prophet is talking to the king of Tyre, but Bible scholars agree that God is also speaking about satan before he was removed from Heaven.)

> *Thus says the Lord God: "You were the seal of perfection, full of wisdom and perfect in beauty. You were in Eden, the garden of God; every precious stone was your covering: the sardius, topaz, and diamond, beryl, onyx, and jasper, sapphire, turquoise, and emerald with gold. The workmanship of your timbrels and pipes was prepared for you on the day you were created. You were the anointed cherub who covers; I established you; you were on the holy mountain of God; you walked back and forth in the midst of fiery stones* (Ezekiel 28:12-14).

These verses make it clear that lucifer was created by God as a picture of perfection and absolute beauty. He was in Eden, which we know is within the domain of Heaven. He was filled with wisdom, richly adorned with precious stones, and God had a ministry or occupation (workmanship) prepared for him from the day he was created. Biblical scholars differ vastly in their opinions on what lucifer did in this position or what caused him to become filled with violence and sin (I have also been unable to find any opinions that draw a definite conclusion, so I will not either). However, I have an opinion about what he was doing that I have developed by placing this Scripture in context alongside other scriptures that address the same subject.

Our Scripture in Ezekiel says that lucifer was an anointed cherub that covers. The other place in Scripture where we see cherubim that cover something is in the Holy of Holies in the Tabernacle.

> *Make one cherub at one end, and the other cherub at the other end; you shall make the cherubim at the two ends of it of one piece with the mercy seat. And the cherubim shall stretch out their wings above, covering the mercy seat with their wings, and they shall face one another; the faces of the cherubim shall be toward the mercy seat* (Exodus 25:19-20).

God is instructing Moses to build the Tabernacle. He mandates him in Exodus 25:8-9:

> *And let them make Me a sanctuary, that I may dwell among them. According to all that I show you, that is, the pattern of the tabernacle and the pattern of all its furnishings, just so you shall make it.*

He then instructs Moses on how to make the Ark of the Covenant, the table, and the lampstand and finishes by saying in Exodus 25:40:

> *And see to it that you make them according to the pattern which was shown you on the mountain.*

Moses was making copies of real life things that he had seen while on the mountain of God. I believe that when he ascended Mount Sinai to receive these instructions, he went up a physical mountain, but he also ascended into the mountain of the Lord's house and was given a tour of the holy places of Heaven. He was then instructed to go and build a tabernacle that was a copy of what he had seen. The Tabernacle and everything in it is a copy of real things in Heaven (see Heb. 8:5). If we then look at the imagery of the tabernacle, we see in the Holy of Holies that there were two cherubs whose wings were to cover the mercy seat (see Exod. 25:19-20). The mercy seat was on top of the Ark of the Covenant and it was the place where God said He would meet with Moses.

> *And there I will meet with you, and I will speak with you from above the mercy seat, from between the two cherubim which are on the ark of the Testimony, about everything which I will give you in commandment to the children of Israel* (Exodus 25:22).

The cherubs that covered the mercy seat were in very close proximity to the place where God said He would meet and talk with Moses. In fact, they were right there! This tells me that "the cherubs that cover" are very close to the throne in Heaven and have access to see and hear much of what God is doing from His throne. I believe that lucifer, as a covering cherub, had a position at the throne of God.

If he was positioned at the throne, it would make sense that his function would include activities that take place around the throne. Revelation 4:8-11 makes it clear that worship is happening around the throne all the time. Based on that, I believe that "trading" was a part of the worship being offered to God. As he walked up and down on the fiery stones before the throne, trading, he was also partaking in the worship that is an everlasting integral component of life at God's throne. The Scripture records that lucifer did his job well, at first.

> *You were perfect in your ways from the day you were created, till iniquity was found in you. By the abundance of your trading you became filled with violence within, and you sinned* (Ezekiel 28:15-16).

Verse 15 explains that lucifer was perfect in his ways. The word *perfect* in Hebrew is *tamiym,* which means complete, without blemish, sound, full of truth, and integrity (Strong's #H8549). Lucifer displayed these characteristics in the way that he walked out his life before God. But there came a time when all that changed. Iniquity (injustice and unrighteousness) was found in lucifer. The root word for iniquity depicts "a deviation from justice and righteousness" (Strong's #H5765). At some point, lucifer turned away from righteousness and justice. He continued to function as a covering cherub around the throne, but now he was operating out of iniquity and not perfection. He started trading from a heart that had turned away from righteousness and justice. Our heart attitudes are the key to trading. Hearts that trade from sin and iniquity will not be tolerated in Heaven, but hearts that are "perfect" toward Him will have a place on Heaven's trading floors.

Ezekiel 28:17-18 gives us some clues as to lucifer's heart attitudes that caused his removal from Heaven and his position on the trading floor.

> *Your heart was lifted up because of your beauty; you corrupted your wisdom for the sake of your splendor; I cast you to the ground, I laid you before kings, that they might gaze at you. You defiled your sanctuaries by the multitude of your iniquities, by the iniquity of your trading.*

The Bible says that lucifer became filled with pride at his own beauty. He took his eyes off God and began to focus on his own attributes. Perhaps he looked at his own perfection and thought he, too, was worthy of some of the worship that was going to God. Pride turned his eyes away from God and took him down a path of wrong thinking that led to sin. I believe that lucifer wanted to be like God and as he traded with this twisted, sinful heart, he corrupted his wisdom and defiled the sanctuaries.

It was the continued trading with an iniquitous, unrepentant heart that caused God to not only *cast him out of the mountain of God as a profane thing* but also to *cast him to the ground*. Lucifer's heart had become filled with violence and iniquity. He wanted to be like God, and God was having none of it. Lucifer was banished from God's house. He lost his place of prominence in God's government and lost his place in Heaven. Trading with a wrong heart motive is very dangerous!

Lucifer, once the most beautiful and wise angel, was now the enemy of God. Filled with pride and anger, he persuaded one third of the angels to join him in his rebellion against God, and we understand that they were all evicted from Heaven. I do not know exactly where they went, but I do know that lucifer's hatred for God deepened and his desire to be like God grew. I believe he began to plot how he would take his revenge on God. Isaiah 14:13-14 gives us some insight into his thinking:

> *For you have said in your heart: "I will ascend into Heaven, I will exalt my throne above the stars of God; I will also sit on the mount of the congregation on the farthest sides of the north; I will ascend above the heights of the clouds, I will be like the Most High."*

Lucifer wanted to build his own house and his own throne. He wanted to be worshiped just as God had been worshiped. He wanted his own kingdom that would replace God's Kingdom. And that is what he set about doing. The challenge that he faced (and continues to face) is that he cannot create anything. He can only counterfeit what God has already created. In setting up his kingdom, lucifer (or satan as he is now known) would need to copy God's pattern and pervert or twist it to glorify evil. And that is exactly what he did.

In order to establish a kingdom, satan needed his own dominion. Remember, everything belongs to God. He is sovereign over everything. Satan knew that in order to build his own kingdom, he would need to gain some territory in which to establish his kingdom. And when he saw God create a garden for Adam and Eve and give them dominion over the earth, he saw an opportunity.

Lucifer knew that Adam and Eve would not just hand over their dominion to him. He realized that he would have to trade it away from them. Remember, he was a master trader in Heaven. He had spent eons trading before God's throne. He understood God's economy and the legal requirements of trading to bring increase to a kingdom. For him to be legally able to establish his kingdom, he would need to legally trade the dominion away from those to whom God had entrusted it.

In Genesis 3:1-6, we see the first recorded trade that satan made with man.

> *Now the serpent was more cunning than any beast of the field which the Lord God had made. And he said to the woman, "Has God indeed said, 'You shall not eat of every tree of the garden'?"*
>
> *And the woman said to the serpent, "We may eat the fruit of the trees of the garden; but of the fruit of the tree which is in the midst of the garden, God has said, 'You shall not eat it, nor shall you touch it, lest you die.'"*
>
> *Then the serpent said to the woman, "You will not surely die. For God knows that in the day you eat of it your eyes will be opened, and you will be like God, knowing good and evil."*
>
> *So when the woman saw that the tree was good for food, that it was pleasant to the eyes, and a*

tree desirable to make one wise, she took of its fruit and ate. She also gave to her husband with her, and he ate.

In order to gain the dominion, satan needed to trade with Adam and Eve. He needed to get them to legally exchange their dominion for something that he gave them. The only thing that satan had to offer was sin. He can offer sin in many different forms, but sin is the only "product" that he has with which to trade. He needed to make his sin look appealing to Adam and Eve so that they would willingly take what he was offering. He needed to draw them away from their worship toward God and onto his trading floor. In Genesis, we see satan approach Eve and question the instructions that God had given to them. His first step was to engage her in a conversation that introduced a question about the authority of God's word. The moment she responded, he had succeeded in distracting her from her worship. He had turned her eyes away from God, and now he could put forth the "bait" that would tempt her. He offered her the opportunity to *be like God*.

Temptation always draws you onto a trading floor. The moment that the enemy tempts you, you are standing on his trading floor and you have to choose whether you are going to trade with him or not. He is offering you something, but to get it you need to partake of sin. The moment that you choose to partake of sin and take what he is offering, you have entered a trade. You have accepted the sin he offered and now he has a legal right to take something from you.

This is exactly what happened with Adam and Eve in Genesis 3. Eve was offered the opportunity to have her eyes opened and be like God, knowing good from evil. (Never mind that she was already like God!) In order to have this, she would have to disobey God, which is sin. And remember, sin belongs to satan. At that moment, she could have refused the sin and stepped off the trading floor and gone back to what she had been doing. But we all know that she did not. She chose to say yes to the enemy. She chose to trade with him. She disobeyed God and partook of sin. The moment that she (and Adam) sinned, satan had a legal right to take the dominion away from them. Adam and Eve had freely taken the sin that satan offered to them. Based on that, satan now had the legal right to take something from them. He took the dominion of the earth. We know the rest of the story. Adam and Eve were banished from The Garden, sin entered the world, and satan had the start of his demonic kingdom.

Since the time of that first trade, satan has continued to trade with mankind. He offers us sin, in all its myriad forms, and when we take it he has the legal right to take from us. Our acceptance of his sin signals the acceptance of a trade. Every time we choose to sin, we trade away a part of our godly inheritance and destiny.

Did you get that? *Every* time that you sin, you trade with the enemy. Please note that I do not believe that you will lose your salvation if you sin once. Satan cannot trade your salvation from you unless you willingly and knowingly choose to trade it away. The things that he takes from us are blessings, opportunities, strengths, and gifts that God has made available to us as His sons and daughters. He wants to trade these away from you so that you live in so much less than what God has for you. This is one of the reasons that sin is so deadly. Think about it for a moment—when you choose to commit the sin of fornication, you trade your sexual purity for immorality. When you tell a lie, you trade your integrity for dishonesty. When you slander and gossip, you trade the authority vested in your words for self-righteousness. Every time you choose to sin, you have stepped onto the enemy's trading floor and you are eating the fruit he is offering to you. You are accepting his offer to trade. When you eat that fruit (partake of the sin), its seeds are planted in you and you trade away part of your righteous identity in Christ.

REASONS SATAN WANTS TO MAKE TRADES

This is the first reason that satan wants to trade with us. He wants to rob us of our identity in God and hinder our walk with Him. If he can do this, he will effectively stop us from accessing our destinies and inheritances in God. When we do not know who we are or who God has made us to be, we are easy to manipulate. We become weak, pliable people easily led into deception and slavery. We will never become a threat to the enemy; rather, we will be pawns in his game!

There are even times, when man does not value his godly inheritance, that he will willingly trade it away to the enemy. We see this clearly in ancient times when men made covenants with demonic gods in order to secure power or prosperity. Many of the curses we labor under today come from these types of covenants that still stand against us.

Many of the sicknesses and diseases that are killing us today are a result of trades made in our past generations. For example, in ancient times when you traded with demonic gods, they would require the person to drink blood and eat the flesh of their human sacrifices. This is a sin and an abomination to God, but we have partaken of this sin and traded away our honor for the sanctity of life. This type of trade often results in blood or heart diseases manifesting in the family generations later.

Whichever way you look at it, satan wants man to partake of sin as often and as much as possible so that he can trade away every provision, inheritance, and the abundant life that God has for us.

The second reason is that he can only counterfeit what God has done. Satan is not all-knowing; he was not there in the Counsel of God before the foundation of the earth when all the books of destiny were written (see Ps. 139:16; Eph. 2:10). He does not know all of God's plans for each person, nation, or business. He needs to trade them away from us so that he can develop counterfeit plans or twist the ones that God has given us. Unless we trade the riches of our inheritance to him, he has nothing with which to build his kingdom! And he knows it. This is why satan has developed extensive and elaborate trading schemes so that in every generation he is able to distort or abort the purposes of God. When I first realized this, something rose up in me that shouted, *"Not in my generation!"* It is time to become wise to the strategies of the enemy and stop him in his tracks. We cannot continue to allow him to steal, kill, and destroy the destiny of God in our lives and our nations.

IT'S TIME TO BREAK DEMONIC TRADING CYCLES

One of the first things we need to do is stop trading away the inheritance and riches that God has given to us. We do not want to be complicit in satan's plan to be like God. We know that he wants to build a kingdom and a throne to rival God's, so that he can fulfill the evil intent of his heart to ascend into Heaven and exalt his throne above the stars of God. We know that he wants to sit in the mount of the congregation on the sides of the north and be like God (see Isa. 14), but we cannot play into his hand. Satan plans to use trading to build his kingdom from earth into Heaven. We must learn how he trades with us so that we will not be deceived into building his kingdom.

God has a Kingdom, a house, and a throne that is settled in Heaven. He instituted trading and trading floors as one of the tools to bring the increase of His Kingdom to earth so that His Kingdom may be established on earth as it is in Heaven. Satan wants to take his kingdom from earth to Heaven. God wants His Kingdom established on earth as it is in Heaven. Both kingdoms are looking to expand. Both kingdoms need man in order to increase. Both houses need souls in order to be built. The battle lines have been drawn. Who will mankind serve? To which trading floor will they bring their worship? Which Kingdom will overcome? The principles in this book will empower you to be one of those who swings the balance of power into the Kingdom of God.

2

WHY IS SPIRITUAL TRADING IMPORTANT?

Heaven is My throne, and earth is My footstool. Where is the house that you will build Me? And where is the place of My rest?
—ISAIAH 66:1

G OD'S KINGDOM IS IN THE HEAVENS. HIS THRONE HAS stood from time immemorial. His government is established in Mount Zion. These are all places in the realm of the spirit, but God is looking for a house, a resting place here on earth. God wants His Kingdom to be established on earth as it is in Heaven. He created earth and everything in it. He gave dominion of earth to Adam and Eve; they were to be fruitful, multiply, fill the earth, subdue it, and have dominion. Through Adam and Eve, God wanted His Kingdom to be extended across the whole created realm, and He would dwell in the midst of it. However, as we saw in the previous chapter, satan interrupted that plan. Through some devious trading, satan ripped the dominion of the earth realm away from them.

I used to wonder why God did not just stop satan and throw him out of earth as well. I now know that God could not do that because it would be contrary to His nature. God is a Judge. His throne is established on righteousness and justice. The realm of Heaven and all the created realms are framed by His Word and are ruled by His laws. So satan's trade may have been devious, but it was perfectly legal according to the laws of God. For this reason, God did not change anything. He had to banish Adam and Eve from The Garden, but it was not the end of His plan to establish His Kingdom on earth. It was simply a momentary interruption.

God has a Kingdom and satan now has a kingdom. These kingdoms exist in the realm of the spirit. Yet the fruit of their presence is manifested on the earth. Where God's Kingdom is established, you will see righteousness, peace, and joy. Where satan's kingdom rules, you will see deception, destruction, and death. Satan thought he had out-traded God, but God is always a few steps ahead of him. Dominion of earth was lost through a trade, but it would be won back by a greater trade. That same trade would empower God's people to recover everything that had ever been lost though trading with the enemy. The greatest trade of all time would restore to God's people access to every resource that they forfeited in The Garden. This extravagant trade would empower God's people to finish the work of Kingdom expansion that was interrupted so many generations ago.

Today, in the earth, there are still two kingdoms, two houses, two trading floors. Both are expanding every day due to the actions of men and women like yourselves. Every trade that you make builds God's Kingdom or the enemy's kingdom. It is time to become intentional in our efforts to stop building satan's house and start bringing the Kingdom to earth as it is in Heaven. The key to this is spiritual trading. And that's why it is important for us today!

JESUS: THE FIRST TRADER

Jesus is our forerunner having gone before us in all things (see Heb. 6:20), and that includes spiritual trading. Jesus not only made the greatest trade of all time, but I believe that He also made the first trade. He traded His divinity in order to become a man and give His life as a ransom for many.

Philippians 2:5-7 tells us:

> *Let this mind be in you which was also in Christ Jesus, who, being in the form of God, did not consider it robbery to be equal with God, but made Himself of no reputation, taking the form of a bondservant, and coming in the likeness of men.*

When the Bible says that Jesus made Himself of no reputation, it literally means (from the Greek) that Jesus "made Himself empty" (Strong's #G2758). He laid down everything that made Him God; He laid down His life as he knew it in Heaven. It is important to note here that Jesus never gave up His identity as God. He gave up His divine rights and privileges as God and willingly chose to take on the form of a man led by the Holy Spirit. He stepped onto God's trading floor and laid down His life as a living sacrifice in order that all mankind might be saved. Jesus traded His life as God in exchange for the lives of all men for all time who would believe in Him.

Jesus became a living sacrifice long before He became the perfect sacrifice who would take away the sin of the world. And the reason He did it was because He wanted His Father to have His heart's desire—that all men would be reconciled to Him. That man would once again have fellowship with Him in the cool of the day. Jesus traded His life so that His father's joy could be complete.

> *Looking unto Jesus, the author and finisher of our faith, who for the joy that was set before Him endured the cross, despising the shame, and has sat down at the right hand of the throne of God* (Hebrews 12:2).

Jesus traded with great joy in His heart. The sacrifice was tough, but the trade won a great victory for his Father and His Kingdom. His trade ensured that man would again have access to eternal life, divine health, creativity, and all the resources of Heaven that were available to Adam in The Garden. Jesus made the trade so that we would be empowered to fulfill the original mandate given to Adam in The Garden—to be fruitful, multiply, fill the earth, subdue it, and have dominion over it! His trade kicked off a new era of Kingdom expansion. It is our job to continue what He began. Learning how to trade in the heavenly realm is an important first step.

REVERSING DEMONIC TRADES TO RECOVER LOST BLESSINGS

Satan has used trading to legally remove blessing, provision, and even destiny from our lives. Just as with Eve, satan has used sin to entice people to step onto his trading floor and trade with him since the beginning of time. This means that each time that we stepped onto the enemy's trading floor, *we* traded away our own blessings and breakthroughs. We probably did not perceive what we were doing at the time, but ignorance is not a valid defense in the courts of Heaven. And because we have not understood spiritual trading, satan has steadfastly been stealing from us and our families, often for generations. I believe that many of our ancestors traded away inheritances that were assigned to our family lines by God. It is safe to say that our ignorance of spiritual trading has afforded the enemy ample opportunity to amass a huge treasury of wealth and resources that were intended for God's people.

Our sin, transgressions, and iniquities are what have given the enemy legal right to take these blessings from us and our ancestors. Before the cross, that legal right stood against us in the court of Heaven and was the reason that the enemy could hold on to all our stuff. But Jesus' trade at the cross changed all that. His redeeming sacrifice erased the enemy's legal rights against us. Colossians 2:13-15 says:

> *Having forgiven you all trespasses, having wiped out the handwriting of requirements that was against us, which was contrary to us. And He has taken it out of the way, having nailed it to the cross. Having disarmed principalities and powers, He made a public spectacle of them, triumphing over them in it.*

The work of the cross reversed every curse and overcame every sickness, disease, and poverty. The blood of Jesus has the power to annul every trade, defeat every enemy, and redeem every purpose for which we were created.

Jesus made the trade. He paid the price so that we can claim back everything that has been taken. And that is the point—we need to claim it back. The enemy does not just return everything that was stolen. He is a liar and a thief. He keeps holding on to it until we come and lay a legal claim to get it back. He knows that Jesus nullified the trade. He knows that the blood of Jesus removed the legal right that allowed him to take your blessings, but he wants to know if you know. He wants to know if *you know* what the blood of Jesus really did for you. So he waits and he holds on to your inheritance, your breakthrough, your provision, your destiny.

I am convinced that God's people perish for lack of knowledge (see Hos. 4:6). Many of us are struggling to survive. We do not seem to live as overcomers in Christ. We are not walking in the fruitfulness and abundance that we know is ours in Christ. Why not? We have too little knowledge of the ways of God. We are passive believers. We have not understood that we have to appropriate what Jesus did at the cross. We thought it was all done. We thought we could just sit back and life would just come into order because we accepted Christ. Well, no!

Jesus's trade at the cross was complete. It was all-encompassing. Nothing was left undone. He is now seated at the right hand of the Father, waiting. Waiting for what? Hebrews 10:12-13 says:

> *But this Man, after He had offered one sacrifice for sins forever, sat down at the right hand of God, from that time waiting till His enemies are made His footstool.*

Jesus' trade at the cross broke the power of the enemy. He did His part. He is now waiting *for us* to appropriate His work. He is waiting for us to take His victory and apply it in our lives and our nations so that His enemies can be put under His feet. Jesus *made* the ultimate trade, but we need to learn how to *apply* that trade. Without a good understanding of spiritual trading, you will not be able to recover all that has been lost and stolen from you.

SPIRITUAL TRADING BRINGS KINGDOM EXPANSION

We have seen how the enemy has counterfeited spiritual trading in order to increase his kingdom, but how did God intend for trading to enlarge His Kingdom? Well, you might be surprised to learn that Jesus taught that trading was an important principle of Kingdom increase and expansion.

> *Now as they heard these things, He spoke another parable, because He was near Jerusalem and because they thought the kingdom of God would appear immediately* (Luke 19:11).

The disciples thought that the Kingdom of God was about to appear. I imagine they thought this because they had been with Jesus and had seen Him perform miracles. They had seen the dead raised, blind eyes opened, food multiplied, and now sinners receiving salvation. They could be forgiven for thinking that the Kingdom was about to manifest, but Jesus purposefully spoke this parable to correct their thinking. He wanted them to understand that for the Kingdom to come, it was going to take some trading.

> *Therefore He said: "A certain nobleman went into a far country to receive for himself a kingdom and to return. So he called ten of his servants, delivered to them ten minas, and said to them, 'Do business till I come.' But his citizens hated him, and sent a delegation after him, saying, 'We will not have this man to reign over us'"* (Luke 19:12-14).

Notice that he only calls his servants. He gives each of them one mina. This is different from the parable of the talents where each servant receives a different amount. In this parable, they all get the same amount and the same instruction—do business until I come. That word "business" is *pragmateuomai* in the Greek. It is the only place in the New Testament where this word is used. It is the ancient mercantile term for trading or exchanging to make gain (Strong's #G4231). It means to do business or to barter. Figuratively, it can mean "to bear much fruit." So the nobleman was saying, "Take your mina and engage in the business of trading to make a gain until I come back."

> *And so it was that when he returned, having received the kingdom, he then commanded these servants, to whom he had given the money, to be called to him, that he might know how much every man had gained by trading* (Luke 19:15).

Notice that the nobleman had expected the servants to have made gains through their trading. He expected them to have increased their mina.

> *Then came the first, saying, "Master, your mina has earned ten minas." And he said to him, "Well done, good servant; because you were faithful in a very little, have authority over ten cities." And the second came, saying, "Master, your mina has earned five minas." Likewise he said to him, "You also be over five cities."*
>
> *Then another came, saying, "Master, here is your mina, which I have kept put away in a handkerchief. For I feared you, because you are an austere man. You collect what you did not*

deposit, and reap what you did not sow." And he said to him, "Out of your own mouth I will judge you, you wicked servant. You knew that I was an austere man, collecting what I did not deposit and reaping what I did not sow. Why then did you not put my money in the bank, that at my coming I might have collected it with interest?"

And he said to those who stood by, "Take the mina from him, and give it to him who has ten minas." (But they said to him, "Master, he has ten minas.") "For I say to you, that to everyone who has will be given; and from him who does not have, even what he has will be taken away from him. But bring here those enemies of mine, who did not want me to reign over them, and slay them before me" (Luke 19:16-27).

In this parable, the nobleman represents Jesus, and He is educating the disciples on what will happen before the Kingdom is established. Here are some key ideas that are laid out in this parable.

Trading Is Not for Everyone

The nobleman only calls the servants and gives the minas to them. These are those who are already serving in his house. They are in submission to the master and can be entrusted to take care of his finances (his economy) while he is away. The citizens, those who are not a part of his household, represent those who are not of the household of God. It says that they hate the nobleman and refuse to be ruled by him. That sounds like unbelievers to me—those who hate God and refuse to submit to Him. They are not given anything by the nobleman when he leaves. They cannot trade for him and have no part in his economy.

Everybody Starts Trading with the Same Amount

He gives each of the servants one mina. A mina is a unit of weight (roughly 1.25 pounds) and also a unit of currency that equated to 100 drachmae in ancient Greece. I have not been able to find an accurate equation of how much that would be by today's standards, but suffice to say that it was not a huge amount of money. (Different writings have it between $17 and $35.) The main point is that everyone receives the same portion. One mina.

I believe that the mina represents the life that Jesus died to give us. The life that He won for us at the cross. When we are born again we all receive life. The life we get is exactly the same. We all start in the same place when we are born again. We all receive the same "hope of glory" in seed form. No matter who you are and no matter what your life was like before, when you are born again you have access to the same riches and inheritance as any other born-again person.

> *There is neither Jew nor Greek, there is neither slave nor free, there is neither male nor female; for you are all one in Christ Jesus* (Galatians 3:28).

It is how you chose to trade with that life that defines you in the Kingdom.

Faithfulness with a Little

The nobleman rewards the first servant with authority over ten cities because he was faithful with little. This is a very important key to trading. We have to start with what we have. When I talk about trading, people always say to me, "Well, I do not have anything with which to trade. I am not good at anything, I have no money, I have nothing to give." That is simply not true. That is the voice of one who does not really know how to value what they have in their hand. God's principle is that if you are faithful with a little, He will give you more. Most of us never get to be faithful with little because we never start being faithful. We never have eyes to see what He has already placed within us. Even if it is something as small and insignificant as a mina, we need to learn how to trade with it on His trading floor.

Trading Results in Authority over Cities

Faithfulness in trading will result in authority over cities. Remember, the nobleman was going away to receive a kingdom. When he returned, he gave the servants authority over cities in his kingdom. These were real geographic areas with people, business, and economies. Servants became rulers over regions because they had learned how to trade faithfully. The reason that God would reward faithful trading with authority over cities is because those servants understand stewardship and how to take care of what belongs to Him. Faithful stewards understand spiritual trading.

Why Is Spiritual Trading Important?

Those Who Refuse to Trade Will Lose What They Have

The servant who hid his mina in a handkerchief had a heart issue. He had been given an instruction by the master to trade, yet he refused to do it. In addition, he rationalized his disobedience by lying about his master's nature. Notice that the master immediately pronounces the servant as wicked and judges the servant by his own words. The servant's unwillingness to trade reveals a heart that is unbelieving, selfish, lazy, and disobedient to his master. When he tries to explain himself to the master, his mouth is simply bringing forth from the evil in his heart. The master therefore judges him according to the words of his own mouth and finds him to be wicked. Jesus explains this principle in Matthew 12:35-37:

> *A good man out of the good treasure of his heart brings forth good things, and an evil man out of the evil treasure brings forth evil things. But I say to you that for every idle word men may speak, they will give account of it in the day of judgment. For by your words you will be justified, and by your words you will be condemned."*

Based on this judgement, the servant loses what he has. Not only does he not receive any authority in the Kingdom, but the little he had is taken from him.

If we refuse to trade in faith with the measure that God has given us, then what we have will be taken away from us and given to another. But the reward for successful trading is authority over cities. The more increase you make through trading, the greater the authority given to you. And to the one who trades the most, more will be given! I love what Robert Henderson says about this—God is not a socialist. He does not take from the rich and give to the poor so that everyone is equal. He rewards those who work hard and display faithfulness by giving them even more!

The Father is looking for faithful sons who will be about their Father's business. His business is establishing His Kingdom on earth as it is in Heaven. We do this through trading on the trading floor of Heaven. Jesus has shown us the pattern of this heavenly trading and He has shown us the great rewards it brings. Now it is our turn. Jesus has given us life, but are we prepared to learn how to trade with it for the extension of His Kingdom?

PRAYER

> *Father, forgive me for every place where I thought I had nothing further to learn of You and Your ways. Forgive me for every place of pride and arrogance in my heart. I see now that I have been blinded by the god of this world and it has caused me to suffer much loss. I now understand that through my sinful actions and iniquity I have given legal right to the enemy to trade my blessings away from me. Forgive me for my passivity. I repent that I have been slow to repent.*
>
> *Today I humble myself before You and I declare that I want to learn Your ways. I want to learn to*

walk in Your paths. I want to learn to walk up and down on the trading floors of Heaven and be a part of bringing increase to Your Kingdom. Father, have mercy on me. I ask for Your grace and Your truth to be made manifest in my life. Teach me Your way, O Lord, and I will walk in Your truth. I ask this in Jesus' name.

3

WHAT IS A
TRADING FLOOR?

IN THE NATURAL, A TRADING FLOOR IS DEFINED AS AN area within an exchange or a bank or securities house where dealers trade in shares or other securities. Notice that it is a defined area in the trading house. You must be on the floor to legally trade. In the natural, trading traditionally takes place on trading floors in stock exchanges, like the New York or London Stock Exchange. These are physical places where men and women stand on the trading floor shouting out their orders, trading stocks and futures in trading pits. These lively trading floors are rapidly being replaced with Internet-based platforms. These electronic trading floors operate in the same way. A person logs on to the trading floor and begins to conduct business, trading shares and stocks around the world. They operate on a trading floor hosted by the worldwide web. You cannot physically see it, but it is definitely there! It is the same in the realm of the spirit. We access or log on to a spiritual trading floor and do business with God or satan—depending whose trading floor you have stepped onto. Just as billions of dollars are traded daily on Internet trading platforms, billions of spiritual transactions also take place daily. The fact that we are unaware of the spiritual trading we partake in does not mean it is not happening. This picture will help us understand spiritual trading floors, because they are found in the realm of the spirit. We may not be able to see them with the physical eye, but they are definitely there.

Robert Henderson explains it like this: "Even though we are alive in the natural, we are positioned in the spirit realm. We must understand this, or we cannot embrace trading." John 3:13 shows Jesus speaking mysteries to Nicodemus. In this discourse He unveils a secret:

> *No one has ascended to Heaven but He who came down from Heaven, that is, the Son of Man who is in Heaven.*

Jesus declares that He came down from Heaven. Therefore, He is in the earth, yet He is also in Heaven. In other words, Jesus saw Himself living in two worlds at once. He lived in the earthly realm but also the heavenly realm at the same time. This is why Paul spoke of us being seated with Christ in heavenly places. Ephesians 2:6 tells us that while we are yet in the earth, we are also seated with Christ in these heavenly places.

And raised us up together, and made us sit together in the heavenly places in Christ Jesus.

By faith, we esteem ourselves in these places of the spirit. As we understand where the Word of God declares us to be, we take that place. It is amazing, as we do this by faith and take God at His Word, how our experience begins to line up with the Word of God. We have been given a place in the mountain of God on the fiery stones. This is the trading floor of Heaven. It is where trading takes place and transactions of the spirit occur.

The trading floors are real places in the realm of the spirit that always have fiery stones. Through the ages, man has built physical edifices to emulate these spiritual trading floors so that he would have a physical marker of a spiritual reality. These physical structures are more commonly known as altars. Altars represent spiritual trading floors. Here in South Africa, the majority of people know what an altar is and how it operates, but I have found that many places in the western world are not familiar with altars.

ALTARS

Throughout history and across all cultures, the concept and use of altars has been well understood and practiced. Altars are known as places of exchange, communication, and influence. They are physical locations that have been set apart or marked for interactions between the spirit world and the earthy realm.

A dedicated place on the earth where a person would specifically go to bring worship and sacrifices to their god. Each god had their own location that was dedicated to them. Initially, the altar would probably have been made out of stone, earth, and/or wood. As the altar drew more worshipers, the altars became more elaborate, often resulting in huge temples. At the heart of these temples was an altar, a specific place where worshipers communed with their god. We read about some of these temples in history, for example the temple of the god Pan at Ceasarea Phillipi in ancient Greece and the huge temple of the goddess Diana in Ephesus.

ALTARS ARE PORTALS

Physical altars are portals to the realm of the spirit. They are places of communication between spirit beings (demons or God) and human beings. Altars are physical locations where a "door" can be opened between the spiritual and the natural realms. The altar can be simple or sophisticated in the natural, but it is the regular sacrifices and prayers that establish the altar in the realm of the spirit. The more a god is worshiped or called on at a particular spot, the more it attracts attention in the realm of the spirit. Satan longs to be worshiped, and if people willingly come to worship him at a particular place, he will be there, ready to respond and trade with them. The same is true of our God. Sustained worship in a particular place provokes a response from the One to whom the worship is being offered and opens a door of communication between the realms.

This is why, I believe, Abram built an altar to the Lord at the terebinth tree of Moreh in Shechem (see Gen. 12:6-7). It was here that God appeared to him and told him that He would give the land to his descendants. Abram knew that altars depicted places where the gods communicated with human beings. So, immediately after God appeared to him, he built an altar to mark the spot as sacred and set apart to his God. He wanted everyone to know that his God also speaks! But more than that, I think he understood that the principle of building an altar to the deity you serve was one that he could use to talk with God. Remember, both times that God spoke to him it was God who initiated the conversation. But Abram also wanted to talk with God. How do I know this? Well, at the next place that he pitched his tent, he built an altar. Why? Genesis 12:8 tells us:

> *And he moved from there to the mountain east of Bethel, and he pitched his tent with Bethel on the west and Ai on the east; there he built an altar to the Lord and called on the name of the Lord.*

Abram wanted to stay in communion with God. He knew that altars were the place that gods communed with man, so he built an altar to the Lord so that he could call on the Lord.

Altars are portals between the realm of the spirit and the natural realm. Natural altars mark these specific locations. We see a great example of this with Jacob in Genesis 28:11-18. Jacob stopped at a certain place and used a stone for a pillow. That night he had a dream.

> *Then he dreamed, and behold, a ladder was set up on the earth, and its top reached to Heaven; and there the angels of God were ascending and descending on it.*
>
> *And behold, the Lord stood above it and said: "I am the Lord God of Abraham your father and the God of Isaac; the land on which you lie I will give to you and your descendants."*
>
> *...Then Jacob awoke from his sleep and said, "Surely the Lord is in this place, and I did not know it." And he was afraid and said, "How awesome is this place! This is none other than the house of God, and this is the gate of Heaven!"*
>
> *Then Jacob rose early in the morning, and took the stone that he had put at his head, set it up as a pillar, and poured oil on top of it* (Genesis 28:12-13,16-18).

Jacob's dream opened the realm of the Spirit to him and he had an encounter with God. When he woke, he knew that God was in that specific place, and he was afraid because he had not recognized the holiness of the place. I think he was afraid because he understood that one should bring a sacrifice and worship at an altar and perhaps he felt that he had unintentionally offended God. He quickly acknowledged that this was a gate of Heaven. He acknowledged that this was an altar and a portal that belonged to God. And early in the morning, he took the stone that he used as a pillow and set it up as a pillar to the Lord. (A pillar was a type of altar used in the ancient world.)

Jacob erected this altar and poured oil on it. He marked this specific piece of earth as Bethel—the House of God. He, too, wanted the world to know that this was a portal and a gate to the House of God.

ALTARS ARE PLACES OF SACRIFICE

Altars are where sacrifices are made. We see this depicted in Genesis 22:2-13. God instructs Abraham to offer his son, Isaac, as a burnt offering or sacrifice to the Lord. Abraham immediately starts out for the place God has told him.

I want to draw our attention to an important principle here that is critical to the trading floors. When Abraham draws near to the place where God has shown him to sacrifice his son, he tells the young men who had accompanied them to, *"Stay here with the donkey; the lad and I will go yonder and worship, and we will come back to you"* (Genesis 22:5).

Now we know that Abraham was not planning on going up the mountain to sing some songs with his son, Isaac. He was ascending the mountain to sacrifice his son. He planned to build a fire, kill his son, and burn his body on that fire. This was what Abraham meant when he told his servant that he was going to worship. That presents quite a different idea of worship than what we have today. I think there would be a lot fewer "worship" services if we truly grasped the concept of worship! Worship is intimately connected to sacrifice. When we bring a sacrifice, we are worshiping, and when we worship we bring a sacrifice.

Abraham's sacrifice had to be made in a very specific way. It could not be brought just anywhere and anyhow. Sacrifices are brought to an altar. In Genesis 22:9, we see that Abraham first built an altar, then placed the wood in order before laying his son on the altar. We all know the story—as he was about to kill his son, God stopped him and provided another sacrifice for him to offer. The key concept that we need to comprehend for our purposes, is that sacrifices are made at an altar. The altar is the defined place of worship and sacrifice.

We see this truth also at work even in ancient times among people who did not know or worship God. Every village was dedicated to a specific god, and in the center of the village would be an altar to that god. All the citizens would bring offerings and sacrifices to that god for provision, fertility, rain, and even for good fortune. They brought offerings when they wanted to inquire of their god about the future. They brought offerings before they went to war. They understood that their village and everyone in it belonged to that god, and if they angered him he would not give them victory against their enemies. Every major event or season in the life of the village (or people of the village) was marked by sacrifices and festivals to honor their god and dedicate the people or the season to him. All these offerings and sacrifices were brought to an altar where they were offered to the god. Typically, there was a priest or a priesthood who served at the altars, slaughtering the animals and administrating the sacrifices.

Any place in the natural that has been set apart and dedicated through worship and sacrifice is an altar. Any time you step onto that altar with a sacrifice, you are worshiping the god of that altar. And more than that, you have stepped onto a trading floor and are now positioned to transact with Heaven or with hell.

ALTARS ARE SPIRITUAL TRADING FLOORS

All of these activities at the physical altars are a reflection of a spiritual activity. The altar is a designated area that has been set apart as holy and has a structure built upon it to mark it as such. When people approach the edifice, for example, they are walking to an altar in the natural, but they are stepping onto a trading floor in the realm of the spirit. As they bring their offering, their sacrifice, they are laying it on the altar in the natural, but in the realm of the Spirit they are placing it on the trading floor. They are giving it to their god.

A person can step onto the trading floors of satan that are manned by a variety of his demonic principalities and powers. Anytime that you are bringing sacrifice or worship to another god, you are stepping onto a trading floor. In those ancient cultures, every sacrifice was a trade. This is what I call intentional trading. You are not lured onto a trading floor; you willingly make a choice to bring a sacrifice and worship at that altar. You knowingly enter into a trade with a demonic entity who represents satan.

One example can be found in Judges 16:23:

> *Now the lords of the Philistines gathered together to offer a great sacrifice to Dagon their god, and to rejoice. And they said: "Our god has delivered into our hands Samson our enemy!"*

The Philistines brought a sacrifice of thanksgiving to their god when they captured Samson. That sacrifice was offered to their god on an altar in the natural, but it was something they sacrificed to a demonic entity on a trading floor in the realm of the spirit as worship.

When Abraham built the altar upon which he planned to sacrifice Isaac, it was all done in obedience to the Lord's instructions. Abraham would bring the sacrifice chosen by God at the place chosen by God on an altar dedicated to God out of a heart of complete obedience and honor for God. Abraham had no access to the trading floor of Heaven because he lived in a time before the work of the cross was accomplished. Yet God wanted him to make this very important trade as it would establish a precedent and a principle of God. Therefore, He carefully instructed Abraham in how to make an earthly copy of a heavenly reality. The altar with its fire was a prophetic picture of the trading floor of God in Heaven. When, in Genesis 22:9, he placed his son on the altar, he was presenting his best sacrifice to the Lord on the earthly altar, but God responded to him from the heavenly trading floor:

> *But the Angel of the Lord called to him from Heaven and said, "Abraham, Abraham!" So he said, "Here I am"* (Genesis 22:11).

The altar that Abraham built was the place of his spiritual transaction and worship before God. The altar was the trading floor. It was an altar in the natural, but it connected him to God's trading floor in the realm of the spirit.

NOT ALL TRADING FLOORS ARE CREATED EQUAL

All trading floors operate on the same basic laws, but not all trading floors are the same. We have seen some examples of how satan's trading floor operates. It is a twisted copy of God's original trading floor. It may operate on the same legal principles, but its purpose is very different.

Satan uses his trading floor to trade life away from you. He needs to take what God has assigned to you so that he can use it to build his kingdom. His trading floor is cloaked in deception and empty promises, looking good at the start but ending in destruction and death.

God's trading floor is designed to release life to you. This trading floor is before His throne, which is in the mountain of the Lord's house. Through the blood and the sacrifice of Jesus, we now have access to this place in Heaven. He does not lure us onto His trading floor; there is an open invitation to come. He wants us to come willingly and choose to worship Him. Your worship is your sacrifice. God wants you to step onto His trading floor with your sacrifice so that He can trade with you to give you everything that you need to fulfill your destiny.

> *As His divine power has given to us all things that pertain to life and godliness, through the knowledge of Him who called us by glory and virtue, by which have been given to us exceedingly great and precious promises, that through these you may be partakers of the divine nature,*

> *having escaped the corruption that is in the world through lust* (2 Peter 1:3-4).

Notice that God's trading floor operates in truth. It requires sacrifice on the front end. And the sacrifice needs to be willing. God never forces us into anything. His trading floor is established in truth and love.

There are two kingdoms. There are two trading floors. They may operate according to the same laws, but they have very different functions. It is time to learn how each of these work so that we can ensure we are building the right Kingdom.

4

TRADING IN HEAVEN

by Robert Henderson

I F I EVER GAVE A THOUGHT TO "TRADING," MY MIND would have probably thought about trading baseball cards when I was a kid or some form of bartering system where goods were exchanged from one person to the next. I might also have thought about the stock exchange in a place like New York City, where fortunes are made and lost through the act of trading, and trades are made to seek to increase wealth and secure power.

Most people I know would be surprised to find that "trading" is a part of heavenly activity. I was, in fact, surprised to discover that like here on earth, where we can step on the trading floor of the New York stock exchange and transact, there are "trading floors" in Heaven we can step onto. In fact, now through our computerized systems, we can step into this stock exchange in New York without leaving our homes or offices. So it is in this heavenly realm. When we understand the systems of Heaven, we can take our place and make "trades." We can trade not just for financial breakthrough but also family destinies. We can trade for people to come into the realms they were created for. This includes children, grandchildren, family members, and others who are dear to us. We can also trade for the destinies of cities, states, and regions. It might surprise you, but God has given us a place on the trading floors of Heaven where we can even shift nations into their destiny and purpose. For these reasons, it is imperative that we learn to operate on these trading floors in the spirit realm.

You will find that there are different trading floors in Heaven for different spheres. Different levels can be traded for on these floors. They will "open" for us when we are ready to trade on that level. Just like you have to learn how to trade on the New York stock exchange, so we have to learn how to trade in Heaven. The trades made in New York are powerful. The trades made in Heaven can shape lives, the earth, and even nations for generations to come. When we speak of "trading," we are not talking about "buying" something from God. We are communicating about moving into a realm of faith where our passions and desires toward God are being released on these trading floors. From these places in the spirit, we can experience great realms of breakthrough.

John 14:2 speaks of the "Father's houses." Jesus describes them as "many mansions":

> *In My Father's house are many mansions; if it were not so, I would have told you. I go to prepare a place for you.*

When Jesus spoke of the "Father's house," He wasn't talking about a church building on a corner somewhere. Neither was He talking about the temple. He was speaking of the spirit realm and the unseen realm that the Father dwelled and lived in. Solomon spoke of this when he was dedicating the temple. First Kings 8:27 shows that God at the least dwells in the Heaven of heavens. Solomon, in asking God to bless what he had built, declared that God was so huge and magnificent even where He dwelled could not contain Him.

> *But will God indeed dwell on the earth? Behold, Heaven and the Heaven of heavens cannot contain You. How much less this temple which I have built!*

God dwells in the Heaven of heavens. This speaks of the spirit dimension where we have been seated with Him (see Eph. 2:6). Jesus said in this dimension that He called "the Father's house" there were many mansions. "Mansions" is the Greek word *mone,* and it means "a staying, a residence" (Strong's #G3438). So Jesus is declaring that in the spirit world where God lives there are many residences, many places where we can live and function from. In other words, there isn't just one place in the spirit for us; there are many places of encounters and activities we can come into. One of them is the trading floors in the spirit realm.

To get the significance of trading, we have to go back before the beginning of time. In Ezekiel 28:14-16, we read a description of activity that was taking place in Heaven, where the one who would become known as satan in his previous place was angelic in nature has iniquity found in him, which causes him to get thrown out of Heaven.

> *You were the anointed cherub who covers; I established you; you were on the holy mountain of God; you walked back and forth in the midst of fiery stones. You were perfect in your ways from the day you were created, till iniquity was found in you. By the abundance of your trading you became filled with violence within, and you sinned; therefore I cast you as a profane thing out of the mountain of God; and I destroyed you, O covering cherub, from the midst of the fiery stones.*

Before satan was cast out and became the arch-enemy of God, he was a high-ranking angel. He was in the mountain of God and walked back and forth on the fiery stones. The mountain of God is a reference to the realms of authority and government. As an angelic being he operated in this sphere of governmental authority. Isaiah 2:2 declares that the mountain of the Lord's house is established in the top of the mountains.

> *Now it shall come to pass in the latter days that the mountain of the Lord's house shall be established on the top of the mountains, and shall be exalted above the hills; and all nations shall flow to it.*

The word *top* is the Hebrew word *rosh,* and it means the head in place, time, and rank (Strong's #H7218). So the mountain of the Lord's house is a governmental place in the spirit that is over all other mountains or governments. Satan, because of his fraudulent operation in this place he was given, was cast out from this mountain. As New Testament believers we have been positioned in "Mount Zion," which is the "mountain of the Lord." In the spirit realm we have been granted a place satan occupied before his fall. The position satan operated from before he was cast out is now the position we hold in the dimension of the spirit. The place of his function is now the place of ours! This is why he hates us so much. We are now operating in "the mountain of God" that was once his domain.

We are told in Hebrews 12:22 that we have now come to this mountain.

> *But you have come to Mount Zion and to the city of the living God, the heavenly Jerusalem, to an innumerable company of angels.*

But why was satan cast out from the mountain of God? And what does it mean in Ezekiel 28:15-16 when the Scriptures say he walked back and forth on the fiery stones?

> *You were perfect in your ways from the day you were created, till iniquity was found in you. By the abundance of your trading you became filled with violence within, and you sinned; therefore I cast you as a profane thing out of the mountain of God; and I destroyed you, O covering cherub, from the midst of the fiery stones.*

The fiery stones are places where offerings are brought, and these offerings in turn become trades. This is the trading floor of Heaven. Trading floors are a part of the spirit dimension where God lives. We can step into them and learn to function there. They are in fact a part of the "Courts of Heaven." When we move onto the trading floors, we are stepping into a dimension of the Courts of Heaven where verdicts can be rendered based on the trades made. In fact, the trades become the testimony that is necessary for God to render verdicts from His Throne. We see this in Hebrews 11:4.

> *By faith Abel offered to God a more excellent sacrifice than Cain, through which he obtained witness that he was righteous, God testifying of his gifts; and through it he being dead still speaks.*

Notice that God, based on the offering or trade of Abel, testified of his gifts. The word *testified* in the Greek is *martureo* and means "to be a witness and give evidence" (Strong's #G3140). God, because of Abel's offering, gave witness—Himself—that Abel was righteous. Abel's trade caused a verdict or decree to come from God's Throne. As Abel traded what was dear to him, God declared him righteous and Abel gained a voice still speaking today. Death did not have the power to silence his voice because of the trade he made. Abel's faith caused him to trade or offer on a trading floor an excellent and expensive trade. The level of his trade caused his influence to still speak today.

We also see this in Noah's day when he came out of the ark after the flood. In Genesis 8:20-22 we see the first thing Noah did was build an altar. This was a place of trading. From this place Noah traded into the spirit realm.

> *Then Noah built an altar to the Lord, and took of every clean animal and of every clean bird, and offered burnt offerings on the altar. And the Lord smelled a soothing aroma. Then the Lord said in His heart, "I will never again curse the ground for man's sake, although the imagination of man's heart is evil from his youth; nor will I again destroy every living thing as I have done. While the earth remains, seedtime and harvest, cold and heat, winter and summer, and day and night shall not cease."*

Notice that Noah offered a burnt offering on this altar. He had a revelation of the power of something consumed before God. His burnt offering created a soothing aroma that touched God's heart. This became a trading floor. Noah could not in the natural step onto the fiery stones of Heaven where trades were made and consumed. He could, however, build an altar on the earth where a trade could be made and consumed. Just like trades are made in Heaven on the fiery stones, Noah made a trade from this altar and it became a trading floor. Noah, now as the steward of the earth, made a trade in the spirit realm on behalf of the earth. The aroma from this trading floor released the necessary influence that caused God to let the earth go from a curse and gave God the right He needed to set the earth free to produce. Noah took that which was precious—some of the remaining animals of the earth—and offered them as burnt sacrifices. When he offered the precious and traded with it, God traded back with Noah.

Noah's burnt offering we know is a prophetic type of Jesus and His sacrifice. When Jesus died on the cross, He was the whole burnt offering of God. He traded His life for the redemption of mankind and eventually the complete redemption of creation. This is why Second Corinthians 5:21 says He traded Himself for us.

> *For He made Him who knew no sin to be sin for us, that we might become the righteousness of God in Him.*

Jesus traded the righteousness He had gained through sinless living for our sin. This trade allows us redemption. Just like Noah offered animals and their bodies in trades, Jesus offered Himself and His body in trade. Just like Noah offered animals in trade and God set the earth free, Jesus offered His own body in trade and redeemed all of creation.

There is another aspect of Jesus' trade on our behalf however. We can now step onto the trading floors of Heaven because of the trade Jesus made. We, as the righteousness of God, can stand in these heavenly places because of Jesus' trade for us. Not only can we benefit from Jesus' trade, we can now operate on this trading floor. This is why we have come to Mount Zion (see Heb. 12:22). Jesus' trade has now positioned us in this place of governmental authority to make trades for the purposes of God and ourselves.

Ezekiel 28:15-16 speaks of the "trading" satan was doing before his fall. On the fiery stones of Heaven, from the mountain of God, he traded. If we do not read this carefully, we might think there is something wrong with trading. The problem, however, was not with trading but with the condition of the heart involved in trading! There was iniquity in him and impurity in his heart. His motive in trading was what was wrong. The heart connected to the trading is what is important as we will find that trading is a big part of transactions in the spirit realm.

Jesus addressed how important it is to stand on trading floors with a right heart. In Matthew 5:23-26 we see Jesus cautioning about making trades or offerings with a wrong heart.

> *Therefore if you bring your gift to the altar, and there remember that your brother has something against you, leave your gift there before the altar, and go your way. First be reconciled to your brother, and then come and offer your gift. Agree with your adversary quickly, while you are on the way with him, lest your adversary deliver you to the judge, the judge hand you over*

to the officer, and you be thrown into prison. Assuredly, I say to you, you will by no means get out of there till you have paid the last penny.

If we bring an offering and remember there is a problem with someone, we are to leave our gift and get it corrected. Jesus was saying we are not to bring an offering with a defiled heart of bitterness, anger, unforgiveness, or hatred. To do so is to risk being judged and thrown into prison in the spirit realm. The reason is our offerings/trades carry the condition, sound, and testimony of our hearts. If we bring an offering with these issues in our hearts, our adversary the devil will use this evidence before the Judge. The Judge will have no alternative than to allow us to be thrown into prison and suffer the consequences.

To understand this we must know the word *adversary* is the Greek word *antidikos*. It means "one who brings a lawsuit" (Strong's #G476). A lawsuit can only be brought with evidence to back it up. The sound/testimony attached to our offerings in the spirit realm can provide the evidence needed to bring the lawsuit. The devil presents this before the legal realm of the spirit or the Courts of Heaven. He makes his case against us. The Judge has no alternative than to sentence us to prison in the spirit. This is why Jesus warned against bringing an offering or making a trade with an impure heart. This is what satan did while he was still in Heaven. The result was he lost his place in the mountain of God and from the fiery stones, the trading floors of Heaven. He lost his right to trade in this dimension. We too must learn how to make trades in the spirit world. God has given us the right because of the offering of His Son Jesus to stand in this dimension. From this place in the spirit we can trade. The result can be breakthrough for our families and us. It can also result in even nations being freed into their destiny when we operate as the governmental people of God.

There is a great mystery concerning trading. Let's continue and discover some of God's ways and begin to work with Him. The results could be phenomenal.

5

TRADING WITH THE ENEMY

I HAVE SEEN THAT ONE CAN TRADE INTENTIONALLY OR unintentionally. Unintentional trading happens when we simply do not understand the spiritual dynamics of a given situation. We are unaware that our physical actions are having a spiritual consequence. I believe this happens quite frequently because we are poorly educated in the ways of God and the principles of the heavenly realm. Scripture says in Hosea 4:6:

My people are destroyed for lack of knowledge.

That word *knowledge* in its root means "intimately knowing by seeing" (Strong's #H3045). The knowledge that comes from knowing and seeing God and being in His realms of Heaven has, by and large, been lost to us as His people. As our Christianity has become more about the head than the heart, we have lost so much knowledge of Him and His ways that we are being destroyed. The enemy has managed to take from the church much of what we once knew of God, and as a result we seem to be constantly losing ground in our walk with Him. This is not what God intends for us. He wants us to learn to walk in His ways and increase in our knowledge of Him. He wants us to become skillful priests and kings who know how to come in and go out before His presence.

When we are ignorant of the ways of God, we often step onto trading floors unaware. It is possible to step onto the trading floor of God and not know it, and it is possible to step onto the trading floor of the enemy and not know it. It is high time that we stop unintentionally trading with satan and start intentionally trading with God.

So let's start this chapter off by agreeing with Paul's prayer in Colossians 1:9-10.

> *Father, we ask that You would fill us with the knowledge of Your will in all wisdom and spiritual understanding that we may walk worthy of You. Our heart's desire is to be fully pleasing to You, bearing fruit in every good work and increasing in the knowledge of You. Amen.*

UNINTENTIONAL TRADING WITH THE ENEMY

Eve is a fine example of unintentional trading. She was lured onto satan's trading floor and had lost the dominion of earth before she really knew what she had done. I believe this is what happens to us as believers many times. We are ignorant of the wiles of the enemy and end up trading away our blessings without knowing what we are doing. These are some of the strategies (in my understanding) that satan uses to lure us onto his trading floor.

Temptation and the Lust of the Flesh

As we saw in the example of Adam and Eve, satan uses temptation as one of the ways to draw us onto his trading floor. Temptation is a tool of the enemy, never something that God puts before us. James explains this emphatically in James 1:13:

> *Let no one say when he is tempted, "I am tempted by God"; for God cannot be tempted by evil, nor does He Himself tempt anyone.*

God is the one who tests us to see what is in our hearts, but He will never tempt us. God tests us to ultimately approve us. The enemy tempts us to lead us into failure. We need to be able to discern what is a test and what is a temptation. This is so vital because temptation will draw us onto the enemy's trading floor. James 1:14-15 says it like this:

> *But each one is tempted when he is drawn away by his own desires and enticed. Then, when*

desire has conceived, it gives birth to sin; and sin, when it is full-grown, brings forth death.

Temptation starts with being drawn away from your place of worship and devotion to God. It is the moment when you take your eyes off God and allow yourself to step out of His way to look at something else. The reason that we are drawn away is because of our own desires. satan knows what the flesh desires, and he puts it in proximity to us to draw us away from God. Notice that you are drawn away from God, but to where? Onto satan's trading floor. You have stepped out of God's way and onto satan's trading floor. Now you are vulnerable.

The moment that we turn away from God to look at what the enemy has used to catch our attention, we are on his trading floor and he presents us with an offer. The offer is always sin. Sin comes in many forms and satan has become extremely skillful at presenting sin in ways that are appealing to us. Being drawn onto the trading floor is not sin; Scripture tells us that we will be tempted by the enemy. The problem arises when we need to make a decision about the offer that satan has placed before us. We will need to use our will to either accept or reject satan's offer. If we reject it, we step off the trading floor and back into the way of God. If we accept it, we have taken something of satan's and made it our own. James 1:15 says, *"when desire has conceived, it gives birth to sin."* That sin is now accounted to us. It belongs to us. We have accepted something from satan, and he now has the legal right to take something from us. He has the right to bring death to an area of our lives. Remember Romans 6:23: *"For the wages of sin is death."* You may not die at that moment, but satan can legally take something from you. He could take a prophetic word or a divine appointment. He could take your health or provision. He could even take your book of destiny!

I hope that this is helping you to grasp how damaging and destructive sin can be in your life. God loves us passionately and wants us to experience abundant life, but every time we choose to sin we give the enemy the legal right to steal from us and release death over us. Our sin does not stop God loving us (He will always love us no matter what we do), but I believe that our sin causes Him to grieve over the door of death and devastation that is opened in our lives.

Many times, we are not even aware that we traded something of our destiny or inheritance at the time of our sin. With the enemy, you only see afterward the price that was exacted for the sin. In many cases, it is years later when you are struggling to break through on an issue that the Lord reveals to you how a sin that was committed years before was the point at which a part of your destiny, which you are now trying to walk in, was traded away! James warns us of this in the final part of James 1:15, *"and sin, when it is full-grown, brings forth death."*

Stop and just think for a moment about all the sins that you have committed in your life. Now consider what has been traded away each time you sinned. Is it any wonder that we are struggling to enter into the fullness of our destiny and calling?

The good news is that everything that has been lost through sin and trades with the enemy can be reclaimed through Jesus. The moment that we repent of our sin, the blood of Jesus washes that sin away and all the records associated with it. The enemy now has no legal ground to hold what he stole from you. Complete restoration and restitution is now available to you through the blood of Jesus. This is the reason that living a life of repentance is so important. We all sin from time to time. We make mistakes. But do not dwell in the mistake. Repent quickly, get the record cleansed by the blood, and reclaim what was stolen from you! This is our responsibility and our right as born-again believers!

Satan will always try to draw us onto his trading floor. It is one of the main avenues through which he seeks to delay and frustrate us as we seek to walk in our inheritance in God. He even tried to do this with Jesus. In Matthew 4:8-10, satan took Jesus onto a high mountain and *showed* Him the kingdoms of the world and its glory.

> *Again, the devil took Him up on an exceedingly high mountain, and showed Him all the kingdoms of the world and their glory. And he said to Him, "All these things I will give You if You will fall down and worship me." Then Jesus said to him, "Away with you, Satan! For it is written, 'You shall worship the Lord your God, and Him only you shall serve.'"*

Notice that satan showed Jesus something. He drew His vision to something that he was offering to Jesus. He drew Him onto a trading floor. He was tempting Jesus in the same way that he tempts all men. Then he made Jesus the offer. "Worship me and I will give all of this to You." That is quite an offer!

I have often wondered what went through Jesus' mind at this time. The Bible tells us that He *was* tempted (see Heb. 4:15). He must have thought about the offer. He knew that these kingdoms would be His in the end, but He was going to have to walk through the agony of the cross before that happened. Satan was offering him a shortcut to the same destination—or so it seemed. If Jesus had traded with Satan and worshiped him, Satan would have had the legal right to take Jesus' book and prevent Him from fulfilling His earthly mandate.

But Jesus understood the concept of trading very well. He was not going to worship any other god. He was not going to trade on satan's trading floor. He would only bring His worship to the One True God. He refused satan's offer and stepped off the trading floor, His book of destiny intact. And Scripture notes that "the devil left Him" (Matt. 4:11). When we step off the trading floor and submit ourselves under God's hand, the devil will leave us.

> *Therefore submit to God. Resist the devil and he will flee from you* (James 4:7).

Jesus showed us the perfect example of how to resist temptation and refuse to trade with the enemy.

Fear, Unbelief, and Issues of the Heart

Fear and unbelief are familiar tools that the enemy uses in so many of our lives to draw us away from God and onto his trading floor.

How many times have you felt the Lord speak a word to you regarding your life, and when you received it you just knew it was God? You knew the word He gave you was life-giving, but it would require a leap of faith. It would require you to trust Him and not lean on your own understanding or your own way of doing things.

When you first hear the word, there is an excitement in your spirit and you feel like you will be able to do it. (That, by the way, is the empowering grace that is released for the purpose of performing the word.) But then you speak to your friend about the word, and she looks at you in horror saying something like, "Well better you than me. I could *never* do that." Then you speak to someone else and they react similarly but add, "Are you sure that was God?" Pretty quickly you begin to question whether you really did hear God. And the more you think about what He is asking, the more you wonder whether He can actually make it work. Will He be able to provide for you? What about this issue and what about that issue? These may be legitimate questions, but when they are soaked in fear and unbelief they cause you to look away from the truth of the Word and step onto satan's trading floor. The moment that you are on his trading floor, he will make you an offer. The offer will be a sin, but it will be presented in the form of a viable alternative—a beautifully presented alternate option. Something that doesn't require the leap of faith but still makes you feel like you are obeying God. A compromise. Call it what you will, he is offering you sin through disobedience. And if you take it, he has the right to take something from you.

Many times in the Scriptures, we see God's people trade away their inheritance because of fear, unbelief, or other undealt with issues of the heart. The story of Jephthah in Judges 11 is a very interesting one as it clearly illustrates a trade, but I believe that this was not a trade with God. I believe that Jephthah was lured onto a trading floor of the enemy through pride and unbelief, and it caused him to trade away his firstborn child.

Let's take a moment to look at Jephthah's story. He was a man of valor, but he was the son of a harlot. He was thrown out of his home by his half-brothers and denied any inheritance. He joined up with a band of raiders and became an outlaw to all intents and purposes. However, when the Ammonites wanted to go to war against Israel, the elders of the nation sought him out to be their commander. Just imagine. Here was Jephthah, the outlaw, the outcast, and the elders were seeking him out to lead the battle against Ammon. I think Jephthah decided that this was his opportunity to get back at his family and prove that he was better than them. He made a deal with the elders that if he led the battle and the Lord delivered them, they had to make him head over all the inhabitants of Gilead. They agreed, but now Jephthah *needed* to win this battle for his own sake.

A back and forth ensued between the king of Ammon and Jephthah. The king of Ammon said that Israel was in their land and they wanted it back. Jephthah reviewed the history of how Israel came to be in that region and argued that God gave them the victory over the Ammonites years back. Based on this, he asserted that this land belonged to Israel. I believe that this is actually another Old Testament shadow or picture of what a court case looks like in the courts of Heaven. The king of Ammon (a demonic power) brought a case against the people of God. He accused them of taking his land, and he wanted it back. Jephthah was given the place in court to answer the enemy's accusation. We actually see where Jephthah asked for a decree of judgement from God, the Judge in Judges 11:27:

> *Therefore I have not sinned against you, but you wronged me by fighting against me. May the Lord, the Judge, render judgment this day between the children of Israel and the people of Ammon.*

I believe that God did render a judgement because it says in verse 29 that the Spirit of the Lord came upon Jephthah as he began to move toward Ammon. Based on the judgment out of the courts of Heaven, God was going to deliver the Israelites. But based on what Jephthah did next, I believe that he did not really believe that God would do it. He had a legal victory decree from the Lord, but I think he started doubting. Remember, he had a lot riding on this victory. He did not want to be embarrassed in front of his family or the elders. He wanted to prove to them how wrong they had been in throwing him out of the family! In addition, I think that Jephthah did not really believe that God would stand by the judgement that He had released from the court of Heaven. Jephthah was not able to trust in the Lord with all his might. This unbelief drew his eyes away from God and His promises. It caused him to step onto a demonic trading floor, where the enemy suggested that he make a vow to the Lord. Sounds very spiritual and right, but the enemy was trading. Jephthah believed that he was serving God, but he only had an outward religious form of relationship. His heart was steeped in unbelief, rejection, and pride. Second Timothy 3:5 tells us about such people:

> *Having a form of godliness but denying its power. And from such people turn away!*

Satan used his religion and undealt with heart motives to cause Jephthah to make a vow. The vow promised to give, as burnt offering to the Lord, the first thing to come out of his house when he returned home in peace. Unfortunately, when he drew near to his house after the battle, it was his daughter, his only child, who came out to meet him. His rash, religious vow had cost him his first and only child. This was a trade with the enemy. Jesus warns us against such vows in Matthew 5:37: *"But let your 'Yes' be 'Yes,' and your 'No,' 'No.' For whatever is more than these is from the evil one."*

At the trading floor, he traded the life of his firstborn child and his future generations for a false reassurance that he would win. Whatever it was that truly happened to her (biblical commentators do not agree on her ending), there is no doubt that her destiny and calling in God was lost or perverted. Jephthah may have avenged his name, but there would be no generations after him!

The lust of the flesh and issues of the heart, if undealt with, will always pull you onto a trading floor of the enemy. It may be unintentional on your part, but you *will* be trading with the enemy and it *will* bring death into your life.

INTENTIONAL TRADING WITH THE ENEMY

This type of trading is done when a person deliberately engages with the enemy. A person willingly brings a sacrifice to another god in order to gain something from that god. Intentional trading is seen very clearly in our history. As I explained before, ancient cultures believed that the gods were the ones who ruled the earth. They understood that the earth realm was governed by the rulers of the spirit realm. This was why every tribe and every village was dedicated to a god (demonic entity). The people of the tribe looked to this god to provide for them, protect them, and watch over them. These gods were worshiped with regular offerings and sacrifices administered by the priests. When a tribe went to war, they believed that it was their god who would deliver victory or defeat. For this reason, they always brought a sacrifice to their god before going to war. These offerings were sacrifices that involved the shedding of blood. The offering always had to have blood because the life is in the blood (see Lev. 17:11), and they understood that bloodshed strengthened their god. They traded their earthly life as a sacrifice on the altar so that their god could be strengthened to deliver them. The greater the bloodshed or the more pure and innocent the sacrifice, the greater the power released. This is why many of the tribes would offer young virgins as sacrifice. This is why the god Molech required that children be offered to him. When the priests took the children or the young girls, they would slaughter them on the altar and offer the sacrifice to their god. They did it in the natural, but they were stepping onto a trading floor in the realm of the spirit and trading the lives of people for victory.

The tribes of old also made covenants with their gods in order to assure victory in war. They would promise to give the god all their firstborn children if he would give them victory over their enemies. They would then offer a firstborn child on the altar of the god so that blood would be shed to ratify the spiritual covenant that had been made between the god and the tribe. This is more than a simple trade; this is a legal agreement in the realm of the spirit. It operates on the same principle as trading, and it is recorded legally and sealed with blood. These spiritual blood covenants are very real and still stand today against the people who carry the DNA of the tribe that made the covenant.

What that means for you is that you may be a firstborn child and you just cannot seem to break through in your life. Everything you turn your hand to fails. Or you just keep getting mixed up with the wrong people and getting into bad situations, no matter what you do. It could be that your ancestors entered into a covenant as I described above and the enemy is laying claim to your life as part of his legal trade. Your life belongs to the enemy because your ancestors traded it to him in a legal trade many years ago. Trading takes place in the realm of the spirit where there is no time. It is for this reason that trades made centuries ago can still affect you today. Sometimes, the challenges we face are not of our own making but are a result of trades made in our bloodline years ago.

If you are a firstborn and suspect that this may have happened in your bloodline, why don't you pray right now?

> *Father, I want to come and repent on behalf of anyone in my bloodline on my mother's side and my father's side who intentionally entered into a trade to dedicate their firstborn child to another god. I repent for agreeing to enter into such a trade. I repent for any blood rituals that were done and any sacrifices that were made in order to ratify this agreement. I call these actions sin. I ask that You would forgive us for doing these terrible things. We have sinned against You, God.*
>
> *Father, my ancestors did not know You, and they made these agreements and covenants out of fear and pride. Father, I want to repent for these heart motives because I believe that if I was in their situation I would do the same. I repent for every place where we made this "firstborn" covenant because we were afraid. We were in fear for our lives and we did not know You. I repent for every place where we chose to trust and make covenant with other gods to protect us and provide for us. I ask that You would forgive us. I repent for the unbelief in my heart that causes us to make covenants with other gods in order to make us strong and victorious in battle. I repent that we did not look to You but*

> *chose to make covenant with another god. Father, forgive us.*

(If you sense any further heart motive in your spirit, go ahead and repent of that right now.)

> *I declare today that as for me and my house we have chosen to serve the Lord, the Living God Almighty. I renounce this firstborn covenant and say I want no part of it. I make this declaration for myself and for my generations into the future. I give back everything that I gained out of this covenant—all the wealth, influence, power, protection, provision, and anything else. I give it back. I want nothing of the enemy's. I only want what comes to me from the hand of Father God.*

You would now seek to bring your case in the court asking for this decree:

> *I ask that the firstborn blood covenant between my ancestors and this other god would now be nailed to the cross according to Colossians 2:14. I ask that the covenant would be annulled in the court of Heaven based on the finished work of Jesus at the cross. I ask that every place where the enemy has been holding my destiny captive or delaying my progress, he would be arrested and a full restoration of what has been written in my book would be released.*

Once you are in the court, you would obviously need to answer any further accusation with repentance until you can secure this decree for yourself and your generations to come. There has been a lot of intentional trading in our bloodlines, but every trade has been nullified through Jesus' work on the cross, and you can use this same type of prayer each time God reveals an issue to you.

Now, we know that this happened among our ancestors very frequently, but as born-again believers we should not intentionally be trading with the enemy. However, the enemy is quite adept at deceiving us into trading with him. There are times when believers happily partake in demonic trades because they do not realize what they are doing. I want to point out that just because you do not know what you are doing, that does not mean the trade is unintentional. As explained earlier, unintentional trade is based on temptation and hidden heart issues. Intentional trading is when the trade is premeditated. The person goes to an altar and willingly gives their sacrifice in order to receive something from the god of that altar. Their heart has deceived them into believing that what they are doing is harmless and so they have no idea that they are trading. Let me give you an example.

Fortune-telling

People go to fortune-tellers because they are seeking information about their lives. People do it for many reasons. Unbelievers frequent fortune-tellers because they do not know God and are looking for reassurance regarding their futures.

Some people, even Christians, do it for fun—to see if the medium can tell them something they do not know. Whatever the reason, a person needs to pay a sum of money to the medium to retrieve information from the realm of the spirit for them. The person provides finance in return for information. This is a trade. But it is a trade with the enemy, and he does not play fair.

Here is a simple example. In the natural, a man (let's call him Fred) wanted to know what the future held for him. He went down to his local psychic (let's call her Madame Zorba) to help him. He paid her a sum of money, and she did a ritual (from chanting to looking into a glass ball to throwing bones), after which she gave Fred some information about his future. Fred thanked her and left and thought that was the end of the story. What Fred did not understand as that he just stepped onto a trading floor and traded with the enemy. Let's break this trade down to understand what happened in the realm of the spirit.

Fred wants information that he cannot access on his own. He seeks out a person who is known to have access to such intelligence. Madame Zorba is a psychic, a priest if you will, who worships a demonic entity. She has established an altar at her place of business. It is a defined area where she communes with her god and his spirit guides. As a priest, she administrates the offerings or sacrifices of people who come to her altar to inquire of her god. When Fred comes to see her, he brings an offering. The sum of money that he pays to see Madame Zorba is actually an offering. It is the payment that must be made in order to trade for information. His offering is received at Madame Zorba's altar, and she gives it as a sacrifice to her god. The moment that happens, she steps onto a trading floor and trades Fred's offering for the information. The information is duly released to her by a demonic entity and she passes it along to Fred.

We need to understand that very often this information is accurate, but it has been corrupted. Words are like seed. They are planted in human beings and grow up to take on the form of that word. Words that are released from demonic trading floors are not whole and integral. They carry the fingerprints of satan, who is the father of lies. So the word might look good at the outset, but it grows up in the person's life to be a twisted, perverted copy of the true word. This is the true cost of the trade that Fred made. The enemy comes only to lie, steal, and destroy—there is no good thing in him. Life can never come out of any trade with him.

It is also important to note that there is another ramification of such a trade. When Fred gave his offering to Madam Zorba, he gave her permission to look into and access his life. He asked her to look at his future. Now, we know that our futures are written in our books of destiny. Fred actually gave Madame Zorba (and the demonic entities behind her) the legal right to access his book of destiny. If he was holding it before this encounter, you can be sure that he lost it during this trade. How? Well, he gave her his permission to access the book and read it. At no point did he revoke that permission, and the enemy will never return what he does not have to return. In addition to the enemy having unfettered access to Fred's book of destiny, he also has ongoing access to speak into Fred's life. The access granted and the permission to release information into his life was also never revoked, so the enemy has a portal through which he can now trade information in and out of your life. A quick visit to the fortune-teller for laughs is not looking so funny now! Let's look at another example of intentional trading that you might never have considered.

Gambling

There are people who would argue that I am mistaken in this example, but I truly believe that when you gamble you step onto a trading floor and trade with another god. When you take your money and place it in a slot machine or on a blackjack table or buy a lottery ticket, you are trading. How? Well, you are trading your money for something. What is it that you are trading for? What will you receive from that money? For most people, they are trading for the chance to make some money quickly. They want something that they do not have to work for in the traditional way. They want to make a quick buck. What we are actually saying is that we want to short circuit God's way. We do not like His way, which includes hard work, diligence, and harvests in due season. We would rather approach another god, bring him a sacrifice, and seek his provision. For most people, when they go to gamble their heart is not trusting God for provision but is looking to the god of chance to meet a need, provide a way out.

This is a premeditated, intentional trade. You take your money and place it, as a sacrifice, on the altar of the god of chance. You are trading with him on the "chance" that he will bless you. Your own doubt and unbelief in God as your provider has driven you to make an intentional trade with the enemy. In the moment when you make that sacrifice and you are waiting to see what will happen, the enemy throws a hook into your soul that is a false, twisted hope. As you watch that wheel spin or the cards being dealt, your heart almost stands still, wondering if this moment is about to change your life. The hook of false hope lands in your heart; you are full of hope that you will win and...you lose. But a few seconds later, you reach for your wallet and get ready to try again. Why? You heart has been hooked by a false hope. Your trade has secured a heart connection to the god of chance for you. When you next need provision, your hope will turn to him and not God.

Hebrews 6 explains this concept to us:

> *That you do not become sluggish, but imitate those who through faith and patience inherit the promises. For when God made a promise to Abraham, because He could swear by no one greater, He swore by Himself, saying, "Surely blessing I will bless you, and multiplying I will multiply you." And so, after he had patiently endured, he obtained the promise* (Hebrews 6:12-14).

God has promised to bless us and multiply us, just as He promised to Abraham. And just as with Abraham, it will take *faith* and *patience* to inherit the promises. Remember the reason that many people gamble? God's way takes too long. They do not believe that He will truly provide for them.

> *For men indeed swear by the greater, and an oath for confirmation is for them an end of all*

> *dispute. Thus God, determining to show more abundantly to the heirs of promise the immutability of His counsel, confirmed it by an oath, that by two immutable things, in which it is impossible for God to lie, we might have strong consolation, who have fled for refuge to lay hold of the hope set before us* (Hebrews 6:16-18).

God confirmed His promise to us with an oath because He so much wants us to lay hold of the hope that He has set before us. He wants us to get it! He wants us to believe Him! He wants us to trust that He *will* do what He says—He will bless us and multiply us and do everything that He has promised. He made an oath because He wanted to ensure that we would be able to believe Him and hold on to this hope in Him during times of struggle and doubt.

> *This hope we have as an anchor of the soul, both sure and steadfast, and which enters the Presence behind the veil* (Hebrews 6:19).

This hope in Him is meant to be the anchor in our soul. The anchor is meant to keep drawing us back to Him when the storms of life have us in fear and unbelief. We all need this hope to keep us on track so that we may inherit the promises of God.

But when we gamble, we trade this hope for a twisted, deceptive chance from another god. We anchor ourselves to a counterfeit hope that draws us away from the abundant life of God and into a place of death and despair. This twisted hope begins to insinuate itself into our lives and can cause us to place our trust in people and things we should not.

I have seen, in family lines where gambling was prominent in past generations, that people are often sucked into Ponzi schemes and "get rich quick" schemes because this twisted, misplaced hope has formed an iniquitous root in their life. Many times it has joined with a spirit of poverty and keeps God's people locked in prisons of hopelessness and lack. You may not be a gambler, but there may have been others in your bloodline who traded with the god of chance. Their trades gave place for this iniquitous root of counterfeit hope to grow in your generations, and today you suffer from lack and a "hole in the pocket" syndrome. Gambling is trading, even when you think it is not.

Are you ready to repent and reverse these trades?

> *Father, we repent for every time we have stepped onto the trading floor of chance and brought sacrifices of our resources to honor another god. Today we acknowledge our unbelief. We have not truly believed in our hearts that You are for us and that You will do what You have promised. Forgive us for our lack of faith in Your word that says You will provide for us. Forgive us for not believing You. Forgive us for our impatience. Forgive us that we want instant gratification and chafe under Your ways. Father, have mercy on us! Lord, we repent for each time we took a sacrifice to the trading floor of chance. We repent for putting our hope in*

> *another god and not in You. Forgive us. We recognize today that this is a sin against You. We repent and we turn away from walking this way of unbelief and impatience.*
>
> *We also give back everything that we have received from the god of chance including his false hope. We do not want it. We reject it. We trust and believe in God to provide for our needs according to His riches in glory (see Phil. 4:19).*

Once you have completed your repentance, you can take your case into the Court of Heaven requesting a decree like this.

> *Father, the Judge of all, I ask that You would issue a decree that any contract or covenant between the god of chance and myself and my bloodline would now be annulled through the blood of Jesus. I ask that every contract would be nailed to the cross. Father, I ask that You would remove the counterfeit hope that is anchored in our hearts and souls. I do not want to be connected or tethered to any other god but You. I reject every false hope, wish, or chance. I declare today that my trust is in the Lord Jesus Christ and no one else. I say that I choose to believe Your word over my life and my house from this day forward.*

If there are no further legal accusations to deal with and you get the decree, then you would also want to make a claim for all that has been lost and stolen from your family line while you were connected to this false hope.

By now you should be getting a clearer picture of what it looks like to trade with the enemy. And you are probably getting a better understanding of why Peter says in First Peter 5:8:

> *Be sober, be vigilant; because your adversary the devil walks about like a roaring lion, seeking whom he may devour.*

Satan is always looking to trade our inheritance away from us. It is our responsibility to be vigilant and not step onto his trading floors. It is our responsibility, where others have traded with him in our bloodlines, to get into the courts of Heaven and trade back what has been lost by appropriating the work of the Cross. *Every* provision has been made for us in Christ. The responsibility of working it out belongs to us!

The Greatest Trade of All Time

It is now evident that from the time he was cast out of Heaven, satan has been occupied with fulfilling his mission to be like God.

I will be like the Most High (Isaiah 14:14).

Through the ages, he has used sin and iniquitous trading to build his counterfeit kingdom, house, and throne in the earthly realm in order to draw men and women away from worshiping God. Satan's driving ambition is that man would choose to live in his house and worship at his throne. If we look at the world around us, we see that he has indeed been successful. But God has not been unaware of satan's doings. He also has not been sitting quietly by, watching the enemy take over. Years ago, God set in motion a plan that would make a way for man to come back to God. A plan that would give man the opportunity to choose to walk with God again in the realms of Heaven and have dominion over the earth. At the heart of this plan, God would make the greatest trade of all time that would answer every trade that the enemy has ever made. God would make the most significant and strategic trade ever seen that would endure through all time and in every generation. God was going to show satan that, as good a trader as he was, he was no match for the One who created the trading floor.

I know that you are intimately acquainted with the redemption story of Jesus, but let's take a moment to consider His work on the cross from the perspective of an eternal trade. The cross was the greatest trade of history. Jesus traded His righteousness, which He had obtained, for our sin. He became the sin that we might be the righteousness of God. Second Corinthians 5:21 proclaims this truth.

> *For He made Him who knew no sin to be sin for us, that we might become the righteousness of God in Him.*

Up until the time of Jesus, there was no way to recover what we had lost in a trade with satan. When Adam and Eve traded the dominion of earth to satan, there was no immediate recourse. They were put out of The Garden and a cherub set at the entrance to prevent them from going back. The trade had been done; dominion had been lost. The same applied for all of humanity. The moment that a person stepped onto satan's trading floor and accepted the sin he was offering, he had the legal right to take something from them. There had to be a death. The wages of sin were death. There was no legal recourse.

There was only one way to change this. Someone would have to pay the price for sin. If one man's trade brought sin into the world, then one man's trade would be able to deal with it. It would need to be a man who had never sinned. A man who had never traded with the enemy. If such a man could be found, then his life could be traded for all the sin of mankind. It would need to be a mortal man who paid this ultimate price, because it had been a mortal man who had brought sin into the world.

> *For as by one man's disobedience many were made sinners, so also by one Man's obedience many will be made righteous* (Romans 5:19).

God, as Judge of the universe, knew this was the only legal way to deal with satan's iniquitous trading. He also knew that only One would be able to make this trade. That One would need to agree to leave Heaven, become a mortal man, be tempted in all points, and remain sinless. Then and only then could the sin of mankind be imputed to Him and He could be delivered to the enemy to carry out the sentence of death required by sin.

God always knew how to deal with satan. Nothing that satan does takes God by surprise. God's strategies are set, His ways are established, and He will use everything, including satan, to accomplish His purposes. God planned for Jesus to be His ultimate trade to deal with satan once and for all. Jesus' death did not just "happen." It was the culmination of a carefully crafted plan, a divine strategy that was birthed in the wisdom of God before the foundation of the earth.

Imagine that! God made the way for man to be reconciled to Him before Adam and Eve traded away their dominion and sin entered the world. In fact, God prepared His ultimate trade before He even created man! We see this in First Peter 1:18-20:

> *Knowing that you were not redeemed with corruptible things, like silver or gold...but with the precious blood of Christ, as of a lamb without blemish and without spot. He indeed was foreordained before the foundation of the world, but was manifest in these last times for you.*

I have often wondered, if God has this plan all set up, why did He not just send Jesus right away? Why did He wait? I believe that He wanted man to learn how to be an overcomer and willingly choose to worship God. Remember, satan wants us at his trading floor, worshiping him. He wants to be like God. He wants man to worship him and not God. God created us with free will because He wanted man to choose Him. He did not want robots who just did what He said. He wanted (and still wants) people who, out of their love for Him, choose to turn their backs on the enemy and his trading floors and choose to worship God at His trading floor.

For this reason, God did not simply want to give instructions to us as to how to deal with satan and his relentless attacks to steal and destroy our destinies. He wanted us to learn, by experience, who He was and His ways to overcome the strategies of the enemy. Remember that "knowledge" in the Hebrew understanding is *knowing by seeing*. Therefore, God created a living example, filled with pictures or "types" that man could look at in the earth realm in order to know God.

This living example was the Jewish nation, a people chosen by God and separated to Him. He revealed Himself to Abram, who became the father of this great nation. Through Moses, He delivered this chosen people out of slavery and made a covenant with them at Mount Sinai. They would live according to His statutes and ordinances and He would be their God. God intended to display who He was through His people. They would foreshadow on earth, on a small scale, what God planned to do for the whole world! They were to be a picture of the overcoming life that is ours when we choose to worship the One true God.

> *The Lord has made known His salvation; His righteousness He has revealed in the sight of the nations. He has remembered His mercy and His faithfulness to the house of Israel; all the ends of the earth have seen the salvation of our God* (Psalms 98:2-3).

THE PICTURE OF THE GREATEST TRADE

The nation of Israel under the Old Covenant provides a number of pictures for us of spiritual principles, types, and protocols. For our purposes, I want to focus on the tabernacle, the priesthood, and the sacrificial system to see how God painted a picture of trading for us.

When God instituted the Old Covenant, He called Moses up the mountain. Moses went up the physical mountain of Mount Sinai, but he also ascended into the mountain of the Lord's house. As Robert explained in an earlier chapter, this is a place in the realm of Heaven. The mountain of the Lord's house is the place where God lives. After the fall, man no longer had free access to this place. His sin had cut him off (see Isa. 59:2). But God brought Moses into His house and gave him a tour. He saw the tabernacle, the altar, the priests, and the worship of Heaven around the throne. God allowed him to see all this and then instructed him in how to make copies on the earth. God wanted a copy of His heavenly abode reflected in the nation of Israel. The writer of Hebrews confirms this in Hebrews 8:5:

> *Who serve the copy and shadow of the heavenly things, as Moses was divinely instructed when he was about to make the tabernacle. For He said, "See that you make all things according to the pattern shown you on the mountain."*

The tabernacle was a copy of the real one in Heaven. The priesthood and the sacrifices were shadows of the real that would be established in Jesus. We must understand that the Old Covenant was a type and a shadow that pointed us toward the real thing, which would come in the person of Jesus.

> *So let no one judge you in food or in drink, or regarding a festival or a new moon or sabbaths,*

> *which are a shadow of things to come, but the substance is of Christ* (Colossians 2:16-17).

The Law that was given to Moses was to be a tutor to instruct Israel in the ways of God until the fullness of time came and Jesus could redeem those under the Law (see Gal. 4:1-5). The Law was to show Israel and the world that they could never be perfect (spotless, blameless) before God. The Law highlighted man's need for God. God wanted His people to grasp that, relying on their own power and knowledge, they would always choose sin. Without God, death would reign. Nothing would be able to stop satan. Through his trading floors, he would systematically strip mankind of every good thing that God had provided for them. He would take life from them and put them in an eternal prison from which they could never escape. Physically alive, but completely dead.

> *And you, being dead in your trespasses and the uncircumcision of your flesh* (Colossians 2:13).

This is the situation that all men faced after the fall. A hopeless situation indeed. But God, who instituted trading in the first place, knew about a loophole in the system. And He revealed it to His people through the Law. This loophole centered on a system of sacrifices and offerings for the atonement of sin that removed the enemy's legal right to steal from them.

Let's look at the picture of the sin offering in Leviticus 4. When the Israelites brought a sin offering, the animal had to be perfect and without blemish. The elders laid their hands on the head of the animal to impute their sin to the animal. The animal was then sacrificed and the blood sprinkled around the tabernacle and the altar to make atonement for the sin.

I want us to see that this sin offering, this sacrifice, was in fact part of a trade. A sacrifice is defined as an act of slaughtering an animal or person or surrendering a possession as an offering to God or to a divine or supernatural figure, so by its very nature a sacrifice involves death of some description. When a person has stood on satan's trading floor and partaken of sin, God's judicial system decrees that the wages of sin is death. A trade has taken place with satan, and death (a sacrifice) is now required. So often in our lives, we did not realize that we were trading, and therefore we offered no sacrifice. This allowed satan to take the sacrifice he wanted. This is unfair, but it is legal. And you know that satan never plays fair! Sacrifice is always part of a trade. If you want to partake of sin, something must die. You can either willingly give the sacrifice up front, or satan will take it afterward. There is no trading without sacrifice and no sacrifice without trading. (We will explore this concept more in a later chapter.)

With the introduction of the Old Covenant, God empowered the Israelites to bring a substitutionary sacrifice to pay the price for the trades they had made with the enemy. This effectively prevented the enemy from trading anything else away from them. Presenting the sacrifice and its blood to the Lord settled the trade and satan had no further legal right to steal anything from them. As amazing as this was, it was just a picture, a shadow of the trade that that Jesus would actually fulfill.

Remember that the Old Covenant was given as an example for us. These sacrifices and offerings are the shadow and not the substance. God was instructing His people in the eternal principle of trading. They were to walk in this Covenant, fulfilling all its ordinances until the fullness of time came for God to bring Jesus forth.

> *But when the fullness of the time had come, God sent forth His Son, born of a woman, born under the law, to redeem those who were under the law, that we might receive the adoption as sons* (Galatians 4:4-5).

There was coming a day when, in God's perfect timing, Jesus would be sent to earth to fulfill this trade that would rout the enemy once and for all!

THE PERFECT TRADE

Under the Old Covenant, regular sacrifices had to be made because people sinned regularly. Lots of bulls, goats, and lambs were slaughtered under the Old Covenant. God's plan was to bring a better sacrifice, one whose blood would only be shed once for all time. A single sacrifice that paid for and removed the sin of the world. But it could not be any old sacrifice. There were some very specific requirements for the sacrifice that would deal with that first trade of Adam and Eve's.

The sacrifice had to be a mortal man.

Adam was a man made in the image of God, but he was a mortal man who had a spirit, soul, and body. Because a mortal man made the trade, God's law required that a mortal man pay the price. We know that Jesus fulfilled these requirements based on the following scriptures:

> *Let this mind be in you which was also in Christ Jesus, who, being in the form of God, did not consider it robbery to be equal with God, but made Himself of no reputation, taking the form of a bondservant, and coming in the likeness of men. And being found in appearance as a man, He humbled Himself and became obedient to the point of death, even the death of the cross* (Philippians 2:5-8).

> *Therefore, in all things He had to be made like His brethren, that He might be a merciful and faithful High Priest in things pertaining to God, to make propitiation for the sins of the people* (Hebrews 2:17).

The sacrifice needed to be perfect.

Just as the sin offering had to be without blemish, Jesus had to be without blemish. He had to be sinless. First Peter 1:18-19 confirms that Jesus fulfilled this.

> *Knowing that you were not redeemed with corruptible things, like silver or gold, from your*

> *aimless conduct received by tradition from your fathers, but with the precious blood of Christ, as of a lamb without blemish and without spot.*

Jesus never sinned in His life. There was no deceit or wickedness found in Him. In fact, Jesus said in John 14:30:

> *I will no longer talk much with you, for the ruler of this world is coming, and he has nothing in Me.*

Jesus had nothing that belonged to satan. He had not traded with him at all. He was completely without sin. He qualified to be the sacrifice. He was the only One who qualified to be the sacrifice, the payment for all the sin of the world. God knew this. He planned it in counsel before the foundation of the world. And Jesus agreed to the plan before the foundation of the world. The Father would willingly give His Son to be the sacrifice (see John 3:16), and the Son would willingly lay down His life as the sacrifice or payment for sin so that man could be reconciled to God and recover all that was lost in the fall (see John 10:17-18). Second Corinthians 5:21 says:

> *For He made Him who knew no sin to be sin for us, that we might become the righteousness of God in Him.*

Jesus, who was fully man and also fully God, lived a sinless life as the righteousness of God. At the appointed time, He willingly laid His life down as a sacrifice, and God, the Judge of the universe, imputed the sin of the world to this perfect sacrifice.

Jesus, in extravagant obedience to His Father, traded His life at the cross as a payment for the sin of the world. His blood shed for the sins of the world answered every claim of satan against us for all time. His death nullified every trade between satan and mankind for all time!

Let us stop and think about this for a moment. Jesus paid the wages of the sin of the whole world for all time. In this one trade He removed satan's legal right to continue to hold our destiny and inheritances in his house. All that has ever been lost through trading with the enemy can now be recovered because Jesus gave Himself in exchange for us. He traded His life for ours. He made a way for us to have legal recourse against all the works of the enemy. And more than that, this trade made a way open for us to go back into the Father's house. It made a way back for us onto the mountain of the Lord, back to His trading floor. This truly was the greatest trade of all time!

Jesus and His work at the cross was and is *the greatest trade* ever made. It forever changed the balance of power and gave man the ability to take back the dominion lost by Adam and Eve. Jesus' trade gave us the means to overcome every accusation of the enemy, annul every demonic trade, recover all that has been stolen, and restore all things in the Kingdom. Jesus did it *all* at the cross! And now He is waiting for us to put His enemies under His footstool. It is high time for us, His Church, to learn how to recover what has been lost by correctly appropriating the trade of Jesus.

7

It's Time to Recover All

THE WORK OF THE CROSS FOREVER CHANGED THE balance of power and gave man the ability to take back the dominion lost by Adam and Eve. Jesus' trade became the gold standard of the heavenly trading system—both to recover what has been lost and to restore the Kingdom of Heaven.

For those of us who are born again, we marvel at the cross and we know that it forever changed our lives. The cross won salvation for us. Jesus paid the price for our sin so that anyone who believes in Him can be saved. When we acknowledge that we are sinners and choose to believe that Jesus went to the cross to trade His life for ours, then we enter into a New Covenant with Him. And under this New Covenant, we become the righteousness of God. We have access to the realms of Heaven again. We have access to the throne of God. When God looks at us, He sees us in His Son. We are sinless, blameless, and righteous before the Father. We are new creations in Him.

Salvation and righteousness were not the only things that Jesus won at the cross for us. He also triumphed over every power and principality. Colossians 2:15 says He made a "public spectacle" of them. He dealt with every curse and overcame every sickness, disease, and poverty. The blood of Jesus that was shed at the cross has the power to defeat every enemy and redeem every purpose for which we were created.

If this is true (and it is), then why do we not immediately see dramatic changes in our lives the moment we are born again? I believe it is because the finished work of the cross needs to be executed into place by us as believers. Jesus accomplished it all at the cross, but we must appropriate His work into our lives. One of the ways that we do this is by correctly appropriating the trade of Jesus in the courts of Heaven to recover what has been lost through trading on demonic floors.

A CASE STUDY IN THE COURTS OF HEAVEN

It is in the Courts of Heaven that we face our adversary and deal with cases that have been bought against us. It is also the place where we appropriate the trade that Jesus made for us and win back what has been lost. Let's look at a practical case study to help us understand this principle.

Anna is a believer who has a call to the business mountain. She has several prophetic words that speak of how she will have a successful business and be an influencer in the marketplace for the Kingdom of God. She has birthed several small businesses that start out really well but always seem to flounder right at the point of breakthrough. She regathers herself, presses in again, works really hard, and at the point of breaking into a significant level in her business, disaster strikes, setting her back again. It is a recurring pattern in her life.

She has consulted with business and spiritual mentors, dealing with the issues they bring to light. She has fasted and prayed, but it seems like she keeps running into a wall. Slowly, she has felt herself slipping into anger and unbelief toward God. She had done everything that she knows how to do, but it seems that the prophetic words simply taunt her. She cannot get a breakthrough. Recurring patterns usually indicate demonic interference in the person's life. Let's break down the situation for a moment, so we can ascertain what is really happening here.

First, Anna has prophetic words that confirm that she is supposed to be prospering in business and influencing others. (You should make sure that these are tried and tested words of prophecy.) This means that this is part of what is written in her book of destiny. It *is* God's plan for her life. The fact that it is not happening means that the enemy has legal right to resist her.

Sin is the only thing that can give legal right for the enemy to resist you. The first thing that Anna did was to examine her own life with the help of Holy Spirit. Anna asked God to show her if there were any areas in her life where she had sinned and given legal right to the enemy to take this part of her destiny from her. Holy Spirit did reveal some small issues that she had not really seen as significant. (I often find with business people it is the small, seemingly insignificant issues that create great legal access in their lives.) She repented of these issues and set them in order in the natural.

AN IMPORTANT NOTE ABOUT REPENTANCE

I want to take a moment to talk about repentance as it is a key issue in appropriating the trade of Jesus. Repentance is not just saying "I am sorry" and moving on with life. Repentance is acknowledging that I have sinned. Acknowledging that I have stepped onto satan's trading floor and I have partaken of the sin that he offered to me. I have given him the legal right to take something from me. I cannot change what I have done. I cannot redeem the situation myself. But Jesus can. In fact, Jesus has already paid the price for this sin. He carried this sin at Calvary. It was included in His trade. But I need to appropriate that through my own repentance.

> *If we confess our sins, He is faithful and just to forgive us our sins and to cleanse us from all unrighteousness* (1 John 1:9).

I must confess my sin as sin. If I do not recognize it as sin, I cannot place it within the trade of Jesus. Jesus paid the price for sin, transgression, and iniquity. If I do not call sin, sin—then I am deceived and the legal right of the sin stands against me. Too many times I have seen people "repent" of something because they know in their head it is wrong, but they do not really believe it in their heart. Their repentance is just lip service. They are wasting their time, because their heart is not repentant. And God listens to the heart!

Repentance is a deep realization that we have turned aside from the way of God. This brings a great sorrow that causes us to have a radical change of mind about that sin. We determine in our heart to forsake that sin, turn back to God, and walk in agreement with Him. This is real repentance. Once I confess my sin and I recognize that what I have done is a sin against God, it can be forgiven. Jesus *will* forgive *all* our sins. And more than that, He will cleanse us from this unrighteousness so that no trace of the sin can be found in Heaven or on earth.

I believe that we should have a lifestyle of repentance. Our hearts should be turned toward the Lord so that when we transgress we are quick to turn back, apply the blood of Jesus, and receive forgiveness. I do want to add that most believers who are walking in the fear of the Lord do not carry major unrepentance of sins in their life. They are walking in obedience to the Lord and His Word as best they know how. This is why, when seeking to recover lost blessings, we need Holy Spirit to help us. We need Him to shed light on anything that is still in darkness. And He is so faithful to do it! When you are searching your heart out, pay attention to your dreams. Many times Holy Spirit will give you insight into the issue you are dealing with through your dreams.

Once Anna had repented through all the sins that she knew about and that Holy Spirit had shown her, it was time to go into the Court of Heaven. She had applied the blood of Jesus to every sin that she has been shown and it had been removed. It was time to bring a legal case to ask for the destiny that was written in her book to be returned to her and everything connected to that destiny to be returned to her.

Anna went into the Court of Heaven to present her case before the Judge. She based her case on what was written in her book of destiny. She should have a successful business and be an influencer in the marketplace for the Kingdom, but the enemy was resisting her. Anna contended that satan traded her success and influence from her, but Jesus paid the price for that sin in full at the cross. She presented the blood of Jesus as evidence and agreed with the witness of the blood of Jesus in the court. She presented to the Judge that satan no longer had any legal right to continue to hold her destiny and she wanted it back.

At this point, many times the Accuser (or one of his minions) will appear in the court holding a contract or a covenant, which is a legal document that gives the enemy legal right to hold on to your destiny. These papers are where the enemy has recorded generational covenants and iniquities that hold the destinies of family lines. We saw earlier how these covenants have been formed many years ago in our bloodlines. As I said, they may have happened centuries ago, but they are still valid legal documents that testify against you in the courts today. When we see these in the courts of Heaven, we know that we are winning. The enemy has been forced to produce original covenants and records of the foundational things holding the person captive. The good news is that the trade of Jesus has taken care of these legal documents as well.

In Anna's case, the spirit of poverty came into the court and produced a contract that her ancestors had entered into with him. Someone in her bloodline had dedicated the family wealth, lands, and resources to a king. (In ancient culture, kings were seen as the earthly representation of the god that the tribe served. When Anna's ancestor dedicated their wealth to the king, it was in fact being dedicated to the demonic entity that operated through the king.) In return, this king had promised protection, a title, and influence in the nation. A blood ritual sealed the contract. The enemy held that this contract was still binding on Anna, and based on this paperwork he laid claim to her business success and influence.

Anna repented on behalf of her ancestor who had entered into this contract. She repented for the fear and the pride that led him to make the contract. We repent for the heart motives of the sin, because the bottom line is if we were in that same situation, we would do the same thing. We also, through identificational repentance, repent for the rituals that were done to seal the contract. Anna renounced the contract and made a declaration that she chose to serve Jesus Christ and she looked to Him to protect her and give her a name and a place in His house.

This is the repentance that we must do. Again, we must acknowledge the sin and ask for forgiveness. We apply the blood to this sin. We let His blood pay the price for the sin. Then we ask that the contract (or any of the paperwork that has been produced) be nailed to the cross and annulled. Colossians 2:13-15 explains it this way:

> *When you were dead in your sins and in the uncircumcision of your flesh (worldliness, manner of life), God made you alive together with Christ, having [freely] forgiven us all our sins, having canceled out the certificate of debt consisting of legal demands [which were in force] against us and which were hostile to us. And this certificate He has set aside and completely removed by nailing it to the cross. When He had disarmed the rulers and authorities [those supernatural forces of evil operating against us], He made a public example of them [exhibiting them as captives in His triumphal procession], having triumphed over them through the cross* (AMP).

There is *nothing* that the enemy can produce against us that the blood and the cross of Jesus did not deal with completely! All the legal rights of the enemy have now been removed through Jesus' trade. Satan can no longer hold on to your destiny, your provision, or your blessing.

LAY A CLAIM FOR YOUR INHERITANCE

But, we are not yet finished in the court. Now we must lay a claim for the complete recovery of what the enemy took as a result of this trade. We have removed the legal right, but if we do not ask for our destiny back he will not give it up. In Anna's case, she approached the Judge and requested that everything that the enemy had taken from her in regard to the success of her business and the influence that was rightfully hers be brought back into the court and handed to Jesus. And in addition, she asked that any wealth, influence, and business success that had been traded away from the family line because of this contract also be given back to Jesus.

I want you to note that we always ask for stolen blessings or inheritances to be given back into the hand of Jesus. The reason for this is two-fold. The first is that these parts of our destiny have been in the hands of the enemy and have very possibly been twisted, added to, or taken away from. When they are returned to Jesus, He has the authority to cleanse them and restore them to their rightful condition.

The second reason is that we may not be ready to receive all that was taken away. I know that sounds silly to some people, but just think about it for a moment. If the wealth of ten generations were to suddenly land in your lap, do you have the emotional, spiritual, and financial maturity to steward it according to God's mandate? If you do, God will release it back to you. But if you do not, God will not allow you to be destroyed by it. Handing it back to Jesus is safe. He will release it back to you in the right time and season.

In Anna's case, that part of her destiny which had been traded was handed back to Jesus. He in turn gave her a new pair of glasses to wear, which spoke about a new way of looking at things. Jesus was giving her a new perspective on money and business. She had been under the influence of the spirit of poverty for many years, and now that his legal right to hold her captive had been removed she needed to think differently. God took her into a process of renewing her mind in order to be able to steward the success of her company that God wanted to release to her. This process included learning to trade on God's trading floor, something we will get to in the next chapter.

The sacrifice of Jesus paid the price for our sin. His life was given as a ransom for us so that we might go free and have the ability to recover all the blessings He created for us. But we have to do some work to lay hold of this freedom and recover these blessings. Jesus has done it all. He was the perfect sacrifice. He took away the sins of the world. But unless we do the work of repentance and go to the courts to bring our cases, we will never experience the fullness that His death and ultimate trade was designed to give us.

But wait, there is more!

As part of His sacrifice, Jesus not only bore our sin, transgression, and iniquity, but He also took our sickness, our sorrows, and our griefs. He became a curse so that we might inherit the blessings promised to Abraham. He became poor that we might be made rich. When Jesus laid down His life, He took on Himself everything that would hinder us from fulfilling our destiny in God.

> *As His divine power has given to us all things that pertain to life and godliness, through the knowledge of Him who called us by glory and virtue, by which have been given to us exceedingly great and precious promises, that through*

these you may be partakers of the divine nature, having escaped the corruption that is in the world through lust (2 Peter 1:3-4).

Jesus's sacrifice removed the enemy's legal right to hold on to what he has stolen from us, but here the Scripture is saying that His blood won even more for us! He paid the price in His blood to ensure that we have access to everything we need to become like Him. We are to be "partakers of the divine nature." Wow! First Corinthians 15:49 confirms to us that:

As we have borne the image of the man of dust, we shall also bear the image of the heavenly Man.

Because of the cross, there are some divine exchanges that we can make through the blood of Jesus. We can trade our sickness, weakness, and shame for His health, strength, and glory!

Isaiah 61:1-3 shows us another reference to trading.

The Spirit of the Lord God is upon Me, because the Lord has anointed Me to preach good tidings to the poor; He has sent Me to heal the brokenhearted, to proclaim liberty to the captives, and the opening of the prison to those who are bound; to proclaim the acceptable year of the Lord, and the day of vengeance of our God; to comfort all who mourn, to console those who mourn in Zion, to give them beauty for ashes, the oil of joy for mourning, the garment of praise for the spirit of heaviness; that they may be called trees

> *of righteousness, the planting of the Lord, that He may be glorified.*

The prophet declared a trade of heaviness for the garment of praise. He proclaimed a trade of mourning for the oil of joy. He declared a trade of ashes for beauty. This is a reference to what would occur because of what Jesus would do. We can take our ashes and trade them based on Jesus' work for beauty. We can exchange our mourning for the oil of joy because of Jesus' obedience. We can trade any spirit of heaviness for a garment of praise as a result of Jesus' activities in our behalf. Trades can be made by faith in the spirit realm because of Jesus' trade on the cross. Everything Jesus did on the cross was a trade. Not only did He become sin for us that we might become the righteousness of God, He carried our sicknesses away that we might be healed. Isaiah 53:4 proclaims this when we understand what is being said.

> *Surely He has borne our griefs and carried our sorrows; yet we esteemed Him stricken, smitten by God, and afflicted.*

The word *grief* is the Hebrew word *choliy*, and it means disease and sickness (Strong's #H2483). The word *sorrows* in the Hebrew is *makob*, and it means pains (Strong's #H4341). Jesus' death on the cross legally took away every right of sickness to afflict us. He in fact made a swap of His health and healing for our sickness. This is why He bore them and carried them away. He took sickness upon Himself so we could have His health and healing. We also see this exchange in regard to financial blessing and prosperity. Second Corinthians 8:9 makes an incredible statement:

> *For you know the grace of our Lord Jesus Christ, that though He was rich, yet for your sakes He became poor, that you through His poverty might become rich.*

Paul was dealing with finances in Second Corinthians 8-9. He was seeking to establish giving in this church that he had given birth to. I say this so we will not try and spiritualize this verse. Paul was not saying that Jesus became bankrupt so we could be spiritually rich. Paul is declaring that for our sakes, Jesus left the riches of Heaven and died as a common thief and deceiver on the cross. He took absolute poverty on Himself and identified with poverty, lack, and need as He hung on the cross. (Jesus was not poor in His time on the earth. He had material blessings that took care of Him and His disciples as they worked and ministered. The poverty spoken of in this verse is the way He was stripped and the loss of all things as He paid for our sins on the cross.)

As Jesus suffered on the cross, part of what He did was take our poverty. He exchanged His riches for our poverty. This allows us to receive of this exchange and indeed even become rich. We can by faith see every spirit of poverty destroyed. Jesus took it for us. By faith we can receive from His exchange. We can become rich because He took our poverty. We are now free to be blessed and prosper as His children! Jesus did many things for us on the cross. These three are examples of His exchange for us. Through His trade, we become the righteousness of God in Christ Jesus. Through His trade, we are healed and made whole. Through His trade, we walk out of poverty and into prosperity, blessing, and even riches!

Psalms 105:36-37 shows these three things in a shadow happening as Israel left Egypt. Israel's deliverance from Egypt is a picture of our own salvation. It shows God's power and heart toward us in these three areas of trade.

> *He also destroyed all the firstborn in their land, the first of all their strength. He also brought them out with silver and gold, and there was none feeble among His tribes.*

The destruction of the firstborn speaks of the people of God's deliverance from their bondage. The blood of the Passover lamb applied to their doorpost caused the judgment on Egypt not to touch them. Even though the firstborn in every Egyptian house died, none of this touched Israel as God's covenant people. The blood of the Passover lamb had caused the judgment to pass over them. First Thessalonians 1:10 declares we are spared from the wrath to come. This speaks of the judgment of God.

> *And to wait for His Son from Heaven, whom He raised from the dead, even Jesus who delivers us from the wrath to come.*

The blood of Jesus, our Passover Lamb, causes the wrath of God against sin not to touch us. His blood preserves us and saves us from all judgment. We are forgiven because of the blood of Jesus and His sacrifice.

We also are healed. The Bible says there was none feeble among them. Not only were there none sick, there wasn't even any weak among them. This is because of their obedience to eat the carcass of the Passover lamb. When they obeyed the prophetic healing provision of Jesus from His cross thousands of years later was secured. The trade Jesus would make for us they secured through prophetic form thousands of years ahead of time. Wow! Everyone was healed. None among them were weak or feeble because of the power of Jesus' trade even before He made it. If this was true for them in prophetic form, how much more for us now. This is why Peter would say from a New Testament perspective in First Peter 2:24 we *were* healed!

> *Who Himself bore our sins in His own body on the tree, that we, having died to sins, might live for righteousness—by whose stripes you were healed.*

Jesus' trade for us on His cross is complete. Everything legally is in place. We simply need to accept the trade made for us and receive our healing.

By the way, *trading* is something legal. Money and currency are used to make legal *trades*. When we give money or currency to a shop-keeper, we can legally walk out of the store with merchandise without being called a thief. We have just made a trade. Money/currency for merchandise is a legal trade. When Jesus gave His body and blood it created a legal trade.

His trade legally allows God to forgive us, heal us, and the third thing mentioned—to prosper us. The children of Israel left Egypt with massive amounts of silver and gold. Exodus 12:35-36 declared that the children of Israel spoiled the Egyptians.

> *Now the children of Israel had done according to the word of Moses, and they had asked from the Egyptians articles of silver, articles of gold, and clothing. And the Lord had given the people favor in the sight of the Egyptians, so that they granted them what they requested. Thus they plundered the Egyptians.*

The favor of the Lord on His people caused the Egyptians to do the unthinkable, the unimaginable, and the unprecedented. They gave them their wealth. These poor slaves who had walked in servitude to the Egyptians for 430 years left Egypt with its wealth. They went from poor, abused slaves to a rich and wealthy people. This is a picture of what Jesus did for us on the cross. His trade on our behalf breaks the spirit of lack, need, and poverty. It propels us into a place of prosperity, wealth, and even riches.

If we are going to recover *all* that the enemy has stolen, there are two concepts that we will need to lay hold of through faith.

> *The work of the cross paid the price for every sin and demonic trade that was ever made.*
>
> *The work of the cross has made provision for everything we need in order to be partakers of the "divine nature."*

I have talked at length about how we do the first, but how can we make divine exchanges based on the work of the cross? Let's find out.

DIVINE INHERITANCE

When we are struggling with sickness or depression, many times the reason that we cannot get rid of it is that the enemy has a legal right to inflict us with it. We now know how to deal with that in the courts of Heaven. But I have seen that sometimes, even after going into the courts of Heaven and getting any legal right removed, the sickness remains. For a long time, I did not understand why this happened—until I learned about trading!

There are times when sickness can afflict our body simply because of the germs in the air, our immune systems are run down, or, as I like to say, the earthly tent is taking strain! It is at these times that I believe we can step onto God's trading floor and trade our sickness for His divine health. Isaiah 53:4-5 states:

> *Surely He has borne our griefs and carried our sorrows; yet we esteemed Him stricken, smitten by God, and afflicted. But He was wounded for our transgressions, He was bruised for our iniquities; the chastisement for our peace was upon Him, and by His stripes we are healed.*

At the cross, Jesus overcame sickness and death. He won healing for us. His blood dealt with any legal right for sickness to afflict us, and His stripes won healing for us. This means that we can, by faith, step onto God's trading floor and trade our sickness for healing.

The catch is that we need to lay down our sickness. We cannot hold on to our sickness and get healing as well. We need to let go of the sickness so that we can receive healing. It is, after all, a trade. Now this sounds very simple, but it can be a difficult thing to do. There are people who want to be sick because it serves a purpose in their life. They use it to get attention or as an excuse to avoid doing what God has called them to do. Now, they would never say that. In fact, many of them would go around always asking for prayer for healing yet never getting healed. But healing cannot come if you refuse to give up your sickness.

I used to struggle with this. As a young girl I was very ill and my parents thought at one time that I might even die. I was hospitalized for a long time while the doctors were trying to figure out what was wrong with me. In the end I was diagnosed with typhoid fever, got the medication I needed, and recovered very well. But I had learned that sickness would garner a great deal of attention. I did not go on to be a sickly person, but as I grew into adulthood I seemed to get sick a lot more often than anyone else in my family. Nothing all that serious, but if there was a bug going around, I would get it. As a believer, many people would offer to pray for me when I was ill, but it never seemed to work. Until the day that my husband jokingly said to me, "Well, you like to be sick!" I was *so* offended!

After I got over my offense, I took his statement to the Lord and really started searching my heart about this, and I discovered that I *did* like to be sick. I did not like the physical symptoms, but I was actually looking for the attention it would win me. As I looked at each situation more closely, I realized that it was each time I felt rejected that I seemed to fall ill. I was using sickness to deal with my rejection. (How messed up is that!)

Once I realized that, I repented and went to a friend to get some healing around my rejection issues. The next time that I got sick, I stepped onto God's trading floor. I presented myself as a living sacrifice, opening my heart to pour out my insecurities to Him, and allowed Him to minister to me. Then I took that sickness and laid it on the trading floor and I received, by faith, my healing. I want to tell you that I made a "miraculous" overnight recovery! I traded a place of sickness in my physical body for the divine nature of health and healing.

At first I was not sure exactly how it would work, because I was trading sickness (nothing very holy or exciting) and expecting healing in return. But that is the wonder of the cross. He took the "the yucky stuff" so that we can get the "good stuff"! That is what I call a divine exchange!

There is a wonderful example of this type of divine exchange in Mark 10:46-52:

> *Now they came to Jericho. As He went out of Jericho with His disciples and a great multitude, blind Bartimaeus, the son of Timaeus, sat by the road begging. And when he heard that it was*

> *Jesus of Nazareth, he began to cry out and say, "Jesus, Son of David, have mercy on me!"*
>
> *Then many warned him to be quiet; but he cried out all the more, "Son of David, have mercy on me!"*
>
> *So Jesus stood still and commanded him to be called.*
>
> *Then they called the blind man, saying to him, "Be of good cheer. Rise, He is calling you."*
>
> *And throwing aside his garment, he rose and came to Jesus.*
>
> *So Jesus answered and said to him, "What do you want Me to do for you?"*
>
> *The blind man said to Him, "Rabboni, that I may receive my sight."*
>
> *Then Jesus said to him, "Go your way; your faith has made you well." And immediately he received his sight and followed Jesus on the road.*

This man has been blind his whole life. He is sitting by the road begging when he hears that Jesus is nearby. He begins to cry out to Him. Notice that he calls Jesus by the title *Son of David*, which is linked to His messianic identity. Jesus had not revealed that He was the Messiah at this point. So, Bartimaeus has a revelation about who Jesus really is. He is not just crying out for a prophet; he is crying out to the Messiah, the One who made the blind to see! When Jesus hears this, He stops and calls Bartimaeus to come to Him. This blind man immediately throws off the garment he is wearing, arises, and come to Jesus. It is important to note that he throws off his garment. This is not just any garment. This is a robe issued to him by the government that qualifies him to collect alms. This robe is his meal ticket. Without it, he cannot earn money. But he chooses to lay it aside and come to Jesus. When Jesus asks him what he wants, he asks for sight.

Did you see what happened? Bartimaeus believed that Jesus was the Messiah and that He had the power to open blind eyes. Such was his faith in the Messiah that he laid aside the mantle that legitimized and identified him as a blind person. He traded his blindness for sight. On seeing this, Jesus responded, "Go your way; your faith has made you well." His faith in Jesus as Messiah enabled this man to step onto a trading floor and make a divine exchange. His faith in the finished word of the Messiah empowered him to lay aside his blindness. He gave it up. He traded it and received his sight! A real divine exchange!

Divine exchanges are how we recover what has been lost. Divine exchanges are how we come out of bondage and into His glorious liberty! As Isaiah 61:3 says, we trade our mourning for the oil of joy. We trade our spirit of heaviness for the garment of praise. These divine exchanges take place on God's trading floor. The blood over the doorpost of the Israelites' houses was a symbol of the blood of Jesus dealing with every legal right against them and their house. Their exit from Egypt with their firstborns' lives preserved, their health intact, and great riches released is the evidence of the divine exchange that the sacrifice of the Lamb would provide!

What about you and your house? If all the legal rights have been annulled through the blood, it is time to step onto the trading floor of Heaven and by faith make your divine exchanges.

8

TRADING IN THE HEAVENLY REALM

UNINTENTIONAL TRADING WITH GOD

Just as we can unintentionally trade with the enemy, we can also unintentionally step onto God's trading floors. It is not dangerous for us to be on God's trading floor unintentionally, but when we do not discern where we are, we can miss unique opportunities to trade with God and see breakthroughs released in our lives. The enemy wants to lure us onto his trading floors to steal from us, but God wants to draw us onto his trading floors to release life to us. Remember that God's trading floor is before His throne, so any time that we come before His throne in worship we are approaching His trading floor.

Throughout Scripture He gives clear instructions for how we can access this place. Psalms 24:3-5 tells us:

> *Who may ascend into the hill of the Lord? Or who may stand in His holy place? He who has clean hands and a pure heart, who has not lifted up his soul to an idol, nor sworn deceitfully. He shall receive blessing from the Lord, and righteousness from the God of his salvation.*

Every time you repent and deal with the sin in your heart, turning away from the lusts of the flesh and choosing to worship God, you ascend into the hill of the Lord and to His trading floor. This can happen during times of personal prayer or times of corporate worship. The setting is not important; the state of your heart and the purity of your worship is the key. Often when we enter these times of intimacy and worship with the Lord, we step onto His trading floor without realizing it. Our worship is actually a sacrifice, as we are laying down our life and our agenda in deference to His greatness and His purposes for that moment in time. This worship, actually our sacrifice, ascends to the Lord as a pleasing aroma and we gain His attention on a whole new level.

What usually happens when you are on His trading floor, caught up in worship, is that He speaks a word to you. He shares something of His heart with you. We often hear these as prophetic words or we see visions. It does not really matter how it comes; the key is that God shows you something that is in His heart. He releases a little bit of the Kingdom to you. You can now decide if you want to take that piece of the Kingdom and allow it to become established in you. You brought a sacrifice to God; He responded and gave you something precious and life-giving out of Heaven. You now have the choice to use your will to accept it and allow it to become part of you and shine through you. If you say yes, then you have just traded with God. You have traded your life for His. The Kingdom just got extended. A new piece came out of the realm of Heaven and found a landing place in you where it can now be on earth as it is in Heaven. Isn't that amazing? And you were not even aware of what you did!

The challenge with not knowing what we are doing in the realm of the spirit is that very often we are on the trading floors and then we just cut short what we are doing. We finish worshiping and we go on with our lives or the service. We are unaware that we are standing on God's trading floor and He is ready to trade with us. Since I have learned about the trading floors, I have become aware of how often we miss doing business with God because we have no idea that we are on His trading floor.

Now imagine if we could ascend into the hill of the Lord, bring our sacrifices, and trade with purpose—how much more would be accomplished in the Kingdom. Imagine that every time God opened a trading floor we were able to discern it and were ready to do business with Him. I believe that we would see exponential growth in the Kingdom being established!

INTENTIONAL TRADING WITH GOD

When a person trades with intention, it means that they know what they are doing. Their trades are calculated, deliberate, and planned. They understand that an altar is the place of access and communion with the realm of the spirit. They understand how to bring sacrifices as worship to their chosen deity. They understand that when they bring their sacrifices to the altar in the natural, they are stepping onto a spiritual trading floor. And they are well educated and practiced in the art of spiritual trading.

For a person to operate in this level of knowledge, they have taken the time to be instructed and seized every opportunity to learn and grow in their spiritual understanding. In our terminology, we would say that such a person would be a priest—someone dedicated to a spiritual or religious calling. We see an excellent picture of this under the Old Covenant. The tribe of Levi was separated to God and dedicated as priests to administrate in the tabernacle and the temple. They presented offerings and sacrifices to the Lord and mediated all of Israel's communication and worship with God. This priesthood was given as a type and shadow so that we would have a picture of our responsibilities as a priest under the New Covenant. We *have* been made kings and priests to our God (see Rev. 5:10), and we *have* a priestly responsibility, but our service is not performed in an earthly temple. Our service is required in the heavenly tabernacle.

THE TRUE TABERNACLE

Just as the Levitical priesthood performed their service in the earthly tabernacle, we must learn how to perform our service in the heavenly tabernacle. There is a tabernacle in the realm of Heaven that was not made with hands.

> *But Christ came as High Priest of the good things to come, with the greater and more perfect tabernacle not made with hands, that is, not of this creation* (Hebrews 9:11).

This tabernacle is the original one that God erected. Moses got to walk through it when God was showing him how to build it on earth. Moses saw the *real* Holy Place and all the furniture in it. He then returned to the earthly realm and had it all built according to the exact pattern that he had seen in Heaven.

Hebrews 9:16-20 explains the blood of animals was used to cleanse the tabernacle of Moses and the earthly vessels of the ministry, but Jesus's blood was used to cleanse the heavenly tabernacle.

> *Therefore it was necessary that the copies of the things in the heavens should be purified with these, but the heavenly things themselves with better sacrifices than these. For Christ has not entered the holy places made with hands, which are copies of the true, but into Heaven itself, now to appear in the presence of God for us* (Hebrews 9:23-24).

If you have gotten over the realization that there is an actual temple in Heaven, you might be wondering why Jesus would need to cleanse it. The tabernacle in the heavens needed to be cleansed because of the sin and iniquity of lucifer that had defiled it many ages before. As I said before, God's plan of redemption was perfect and all-encompassing.

The writer of the book of Hebrews is clear. Moses made a copy of this tabernacle for the Israelites, but it was to be temporary. The true tabernacle is in Heaven. The Father intended for man, under the New Covenant, to have access back into Heaven and to be priests who ministered in the true tabernacle. It was the blood of Jesus that cleansed the heavenly temple and made a way for us to enter into it. Our job? To minister as kings and priests to our God.

A ROYAL PRIESTHOOD TRADES WITH INTENTION

We have seen that we are called to be a holy priesthood, separated to God. In addition to the Scripture in Revelation 5:10, Peter says we are to be a holy priesthood and a royal priesthood (see 1 Pet. 2). John tells us again in Revelation 20:6 that we are called to be priests:

Blessed and holy is he who has part in the first resurrection. Over such the second death has no power, but they shall be priests of God and of Christ, and shall reign with Him a thousand years.

Even Isaiah prophesies of this coming priesthood in Isaiah 61:6:

But you shall be named the priests of the Lord, they shall call you the servants of our God.

We, you and I, who are born again, spirit-filled believers are part of the priesthood of God with Jesus as our High Priest.

The Scripture says in First Peter 2:9 that we *are* a chosen generation, a royal priesthood, a holy nation. It is not a choice. It is not an optional extra to salvation. We have been saved out of darkness for His purposes. We have a job to do and a destiny to fulfill that is not all about our own happiness. You are not saved so that, primarily, you can have a blessed life. You are saved so that God might have His inheritance in you! That includes being part of a royal priesthood. You have a job to do as a priest of the Most High. You have spiritual sacrifices to bring at His altar. You have trading to do so that His Kingdom can come on earth as it is in Heaven. It is time that we move on from "the discussion of the elementary principles of Christ" and "go on to perfection" (Heb. 6:1)!

One of our main responsibilities as priests is to know how to bring spiritual sacrifices. Peter is very clear about this calling that we have.

> *You also, as living stones, are being built up a spiritual house, a holy priesthood, to offer up spiritual sacrifices acceptable to God through Jesus Christ* (1 Peter 2:5).

We are being built into a spiritual house and a holy priesthood, and we are going to have to bring spiritual sacrifices. But where are we to bring these sacrifices? What are these sacrifices and how can we bring them? We can no longer expect another man or woman to mediate for us. We are to bring our own sacrifices, and we are to administer our own offerings. We *are* priests and kings to our God, and we *are* responsible to trade on God's trading floor to see His purposes released in the earth.

Let's learn a little more about sacrifices and the types of spiritual sacrifices we are to bring.

SPIRITUAL SACRIFICES

A sacrifice, by definition, is something that is permanently given to another that has value to the giver. It is something that we would like to keep for ourselves, but we choose to surrender it to another in order to receive something we do not have. There can be no trade unless you are willing to part with something of your own in order to get something else. Without a sacrifice, there can be no trade.

Trading floors or altars require sacrifices to operate. All trading is based on sacrifice. All trading includes the "giving up" or sacrifice of something to receive something else. If you want a new television, you need to "give up" or sacrifice around $500 of your money to get one. If you want a nice, latest model television with all the bells and whistles, you will have to sacrifice significantly more to get it. Once you have handed over that money, you will never get it back, but you will have the television. You had to make a sacrifice of something that belonged to you to get something that you desired to own. Without your sacrifice, there would have been no trade. As in the natural, so it is in the realm of the spirit.

Just as there can be no trading in the natural without a sacrifice, there can be no trading in the spirit without a sacrifice. The concept of sacrifice is commonly seen in a religious context where man's possessions are offered to deities in order to secure blessing, provision, and protection. These sacrifices are regarded as a form of submission and worship. People who bring these sacrifices are dedicated to their god and use physical things to engage on a spiritual level. They understand that without a sacrifice there can be no trading with their god. Without a sacrifice there will be no exchange. The sacrifice positions them on the trading floor and calls for a response from their god. They bring physical sacrifices to a physical altar as an outward sign of the spiritual sacrifice they are making on the altar or trading floor of their god. This sacrifice indicates their readiness and their willingness to trade with their god.

Under the Old Covenant, sacrifices were prescribed by God in minute detail and the Levitical priesthood was appointed to administer these sacrifices on behalf of the people. Although the priests administered the sacrifices, it was the people who had to provide the sacrifices. Each physical sacrifice was brought to achieve a spiritual purpose. Some of the sacrifices were to atone for sins and others were freewill offerings of worship. Different sacrifices precipitated different responses from God.

God instituted a system of sacrifices among the Israelites because He wanted to be in their midst. He required Israel to bring physical sacrifices and offer them on the altar so that He could respond to them. Sacrifice makes the way open for God to move on our behalf. God wanted to remit their sins, but there needed to be an offering made before He could do it. God wanted to bless His people, but the necessary sacrifices had to be made in order to legally permit Him to do this.

I want to take a moment to explore the sacrifices that God prescribed for Israel as each physical sacrifice paints a picture of a spiritual sacrifice. First, we know that all of these sacrifices point us to Christ. He embodies all of them, and the sacrifices were given to point Israel toward Christ. These sacrifices are detailed in Leviticus 1–3.

The first three offerings are the burnt offering, the grain offering, and the peace offering. These sacrifices were offered on the brazen altar and were given as a voluntary gift to God. They were sacrifices that brought one near to God. They had nothing to do with the remission of sin. These sacrifices were intended to be a sweet-smelling aroma for the Lord that would give Him pleasure.

The sin offering and the trespass offering were sacrifices that God took no pleasure in. He instituted them as a means of making atonement for sin. The sacrifices paid the penalty of the sin. The blood and the fat of these sacrifices was offered on the brazen altar for the remission of the sin, and the remainder of the sacrifice was taken outside the camp to be burned. There was no sweet smell with this sacrifice because it contained sin and sin cannot come before God. As you can see, each of these sacrifices accomplished a spiritual goal:

- The burnt offering: a sacrifice signifying a total surrender of life with nothing held back
- The grain offering: a gift to God of the fruit of your labor
- The peace offering: a voluntary sacrifice of thanks and completion
- The sin offering: atonement for the sin nature of the heart

- The trespass offering: atonement for the actual sins of evil behavior

God instituted a system that showed Israel how they could deal with their sin and live in harmony with God and each other. Each of these sacrifices were physical things that they did, but they signified a spiritual reality. Without the sacrifices, they would not be able to engage with God and God could not engage with His people. This is why, each time they brought a sacrifice to the altar, they were signaling their desire to know God. Their sacrifice told God that they loved Him and intended to live in peace with Him. They wanted Him to be their God and they would be His special people.

THE SHADOW OF THINGS TO COME

The altar that the Israelites offered their sacrifices on was a physical location that had been set apart and dedicated to God. In fact, the Israelites had two altars—the brazen altar and the golden altar of incense. Sacrifices were brought to both of these altars in obedience to God as a sign of their submission to and worship of Him as their One true God. All of this activity around the altars was to point us to a future reality. The sin and trespass offerings perfectly depicted the ultimate sacrifice of Jesus. He was the Lamb without spot or blemish who would take away the sins of the world. When Jesus laid His life down at the cross, He fulfilled this Old Testament pattern and did away with the need for sin and trespass offerings once for all time. There would never again be a sacrifice that we would need to make for sin. There would never again be any other type of sacrifice that could be made to secure atonement or right-standing with God. Jesus fulfilled these two sacrifices *completely*.

But there were still three other sacrifices depicted under the Old Covenant that had nothing to do with atonement for sin. They were the freewill offerings presented by the priests. I believe that these are a picture of the spiritual sacrifices that Peter talks of in First Peter 2:5:

> *You also, as living stones, are being built up a spiritual house, a holy priesthood, to offer up spiritual sacrifices acceptable to God through Jesus Christ.*

It is clear from this Scripture that under the New Covenant we are to be a holy priesthood. Just further on in verse 9, Peter calls us a "royal priesthood." This means that we are priests under the New Covenant and are called to function as priests with Jesus as our High Priest (see Heb. 4:14). Peter goes on to tell us that one of our jobs as priests is to "offer up spiritual sacrifices" that are acceptable to God (1 Pet. 2:5). Stop and think about that for a moment. You are a priest who should be offering up spiritual sacrifices.(Remember, I am *not* talking about sacrifices for sin or atonement for sin, I am speaking of voluntary, freewill offerings that express our love and gratitude to the Lord—sacrifices that are a sweet-smelling aroma to Him.) When last did you intentionally offer a sacrifice that was acceptable to God through Christ Jesus? If we are functioning as priests, we should know when last we offered a sacrifice. But most of us do not even really know what it is to be a priest to our God, let alone how to bring a sacrifice. Many have been taught that sacrifices ended with the coming of

Jesus. He did it all and we no longer have to bring a sacrifice. Well, this Scripture in First Peter 2 absolutely refutes that idea. It is our responsibility to take up our role as priests and learn what spiritual sacrifices to bring and how to bring them in a way that is acceptable to God. And because we now know that sacrifices are an essential part of trading, we realize that without learning how to bring sacrifices, we will never learn how to step onto God's trading floors and trade with Him. Without understanding this dimension of spiritual sacrifice, we will struggle to make trades that see the Kingdom released on earth as it is in Heaven. Trading requires spiritual sacrifices where we lay something of ours down in order to pick up something of Him. As portrayed in the sweet-smelling sacrifices of the Old Testament, we willingly lay down something of ours in order to take up something of the Kingdom. This place of sacrifice results in less of us and more of Him. I am hoping you are beginning to see the great importance of not only learning about our role as priests of God but how to bring sacrifices that please God.

To get some clues, let's look at the Old Testament picture that foreshadows the real priesthood in Heaven. First, the priests fulfilled their duties in the temple. The temple that we serve is not made of hands but is found in the realm of the spirit.

> *Now this is the main point of the things we are saying: We have such a High Priest, who is seated at the right hand of the throne of the Majesty in the heavens, a Minister of the sanctuary and of the true tabernacle which the Lord erected, and not man* (Hebrews 8:1-2).

Jesus is a minister in the true tabernacle, one which *the Lord* erected, not man. This tells us that there is a tabernacle in Heaven. Jesus is the High Priest ministering in this tabernacle, and it follows that we, the holy priesthood, would also serve in that place.

Each time the priests brought a physical sacrifice to the altar, we have a picture of a New Testament priest stepping onto God's altar or trading floor in the realm of the spirit to present their sacrifice. The Levitical priest was engaging with God on behalf of another. The New Testament priest is engaging with God for himself. The sacrifice that the Levitical priest brought was provided by the individual in order to transact with God according to the type of sacrifice he was providing. If it was a sin offering, then he was seeking remission for sin. His sacrifice achieved this spiritual objective.

Under the New Covenant, there is no more sacrifice for sin, so we would never bring this type of sacrifice. But we could bring a spiritual sacrifice acceptable to God that could arise to Him as a sweet-smelling aroma. Paul talks about such a spiritual sacrifice being made by the church at Philippi.

> *Indeed I have all and abound. I am full, having received from Epaphroditus the things sent from you, a sweet-smelling aroma, an acceptable sacrifice, well pleasing to God* (Philippians 4:18).

We see in the prior verses how Paul commends the Philippians for their giving to him. He goes on to say that he perceives their gift to him to be a sacrifice and that sacrifice is well-pleasing and acceptable to God. He explains that this gift, this sacrifice has a sweet-smelling aroma. Paul understood very well the sacrifices and offerings made under the Law, and he is drawing a parallel between this sacrifice and the non-atoning sacrifices that were to be a sweet-smelling savor to the Lord. Paul considered this gift of material provision to be a spiritual sacrifice.

Other examples of spiritual sacrifices are:

Dedication of Our Lives

> *I beseech you therefore, brethren, by the mercies of God, that you present your bodies a living sacrifice, holy, acceptable to God, which is your reasonable service* (Romans 12:1).

Thanksgiving and Acts of Kindness to Your Fellow Man

> *Therefore by Him let us continually offer the sacrifice of praise to God, that is, the fruit of our lips, giving thanks to His name. But do not forget to do good and to share, for with such sacrifices God is well pleased* (Hebrews 13:15-16).

Faithful Service

> *Yes, and if I am being poured out as a drink offering on the sacrifice and service of your faith, I am glad and rejoice with you all* (Philippians 2:17).

We will study these types of sacrifices in a later chapter and look at how we can practically offer these sacrifices as part of our trading.

SACRIFICE IS WORSHIP

It is important to grasp that under the Old Covenant, the individual brought his sacrifice in order to achieve a spiritual goal, but it was also done in obedience to God. When the Israelites obeyed God by bringing the sacrifices, they were indicating their submission of their life to God and their willingness to obey His commands. This was their worship. It was the way in which they expressed their love and honor for God. Under the Old Covenant, outward obedience was worship. Every time a sacrifice was brought, God's people were worshiping Him.

In the same way, the sacrifice that we bring onto God's trading floor in the realm of the spirit should not only achieve a spiritual consequence but should also be part of our worship. The difference for us is that God requires more than outward obedience from us as our worship. He requires that our hearts be in submission and honor toward Him as well. Under the New Covenant, the thoughts and intents of our heart, while walking in obedience, indicate our true worship.

This is why when Abraham took his son to be sacrificed he said that he was going to worship. He had received an instruction from the Lord and, although the sacrifice that he was being asked to make was a massive one, he intended to bring it in obedience and honor to God. I believe that Abraham was an Old Testament figure with a New Covenant revelation.

He understood that bringing a sacrifice was about more than just obedience; it included the heart attitude that accompanied the act. When he built that altar on Mount Moriah and placed his son on it, God was looking at his heart. The physical deed was the outward sign of the obedience, but what was his heart saying? Was it in fear and trepidation? Was he angry with God? Was he doing this under duress? Or was he bringing his sacrifice as an act of worship? We know that Abraham brought his sacrifice with a heart that trusted in the goodness and the kindness of his God. He knew his God. He knew that whatever came of this transaction, God would cause it to be for his good. Hebrews 11:19 tells us that he believed that if his son died, God would resurrect him. Abraham's heart fully trusted, loved, and worshiped God as he stepped on that trading floor. When God saw this, He stepped in and provided a sacrifice.

Each time that we bring a sacrifice to an altar, the sound being released from our heart tells the real story. You can bring an offering in obedience to the Lord, but if your heart is angry and upset that you have to do it your heart is speaking that over your offering. That sound of anger and indignation will be attached to your offering and it will be the testimony recorded on the trading floor of Heaven. This worship or sacrifice will not be accepted by God. I believe this is why God says in Second Corinthians 9:7:

> *Let each one give [thoughtfully and with purpose] just as he has decided in his heart, not grudgingly or under compulsion, for God loves*

a cheerful giver [and delights in the one whose heart is in his gift] (AMP).

When we bring sacrifices and gifts, our heart must tell the same story as our mouth. This delights God, and this sacrifice will be accepted.

Jesus explains this principle of the importance of the heart motive in Matthew 5:21-22:

> *You have heard that it was said to those of old, "You shall not murder, and whoever murders will be in danger of the judgment." But I say to you that whoever is angry with his brother without a cause shall be in danger of the judgment. And whoever says to his brother, "Raca!" shall be in danger of the council. But whoever says, "You fool!" shall be in danger of hell fire.*

Jesus is teaching that under the New Covenant it is not simply the act of murder that has consequences, but the thoughts and intents of your heart will make you guilty even before you commit the act of murder. In later verses, He says the same of adultery. Jesus is pointing out that the thoughts of the heart, not only the act, are of supreme importance. Then notice how He ties the thoughts of your heart to the offerings or sacrifices that you bring in verses 23-24:

> *Therefore if you bring your gift to the altar, and there remember that your brother has something against you, leave your gift there before the altar,*

and go your way. First be reconciled to your brother, and then come and offer your gift.

Jesus is saying that if your brother has something against you, do not stop bringing your sacrifices, but go and be reconciled to your brother so that your heart is pure and your gift will carry a good testimony on the trading floor. Sacrifice is worship. When we bring sacrifices, we are bringing our worship. If your heart is not worshiping God with the sacrifice, then you are wasting your time. That sacrifice will not be pleasing and acceptable to God. It will be rejected.

I am not just talking about financial sacrifices. There are many types of sacrifices that we can make. Fasting is a sacrifice that we can choose to make from time to time. You may choose to offer your food and meal times to the Lord as a sacrifice, so you refrain from eating and spend that time in a time of prayer. However, the heart motive for making the sacrifice is what God is looking at. If your intention in your heart is simply to lose weight but you want to make it seem like you are being spiritual, then you are just dieting. There is no worship and no sacrifice to God. The true sacrifice is when you choose to lay down that delicious barbeque dinner, denying your flesh because you want to spend time with your Father because you love Him and He is better than any barbeque. That is a spiritual sacrifice that is pleasing to the Lord. It is also a trade because you choose to lay down your earthly food in order to take up some Kingdom food. As I said, there are many types of sacrifices we can choose to make, but the important thing to remember is that your sacrifice is your worship and your worship is your sacrifice. So make sure that your sacrifice is truly a sacrifice from the heart and not simply an outward religious show.

SATAN WANTS YOUR WORSHIP

This principle is at work on satan's trading floors as well. Each time that you step onto his trading floor and agree to partake of sin, your heart is in rebellion to God. You know that what you are about to do is against God's instruction, but you do it anyway. You rebel against God and you submit to the enemy. You choose sin over God's plans and purposes for you. You choose satan over God. You choose to honor and submit to satan rather than God. That is a form of worship. And satan delights in it. He wants our worship that originates out of our heart of rebellion! Remember, he wants to be like God. He wants to be worshiped just as he saw God being worshiped in Heaven. He wants to take God's place in our hearts so that he can twist and defile us completely.

Every time we step onto his trading floor and trade with him, we are in fact worshiping him. I believe that *this* is what satan is actually after—our worship, even if it is a false, counterfeit copy of the real. He wants to trade our inheritance from us, but he also wants our false worship. When we choose his sin over God's ways, that false worship that we are giving him is used to build his kingdom. I believe that our false worship strengthens his hold on the kingdoms of this world. It is an integral part of his trading system, just as spiritual sacrifices and worship are an integral part of God's trading floor.

It is time to get off satan's trading floor. It is time to stop offering him false worship and come into the place of true worship. It is time to stop building the enemy's house. It is time to be built into God's spiritual house and to become His holy priesthood that offers spiritual sacrifices that are acceptable to Him in Christ Jesus.

Let's take a moment and repent.

> *Father, I realize today that each time I chose to sin against You, I was also choosing to worship satan. I repent. I repent for choosing his ways over Your ways. I repent for the rebellion in my heart that does not want to submit to Your instruction. I repent that many times I may have outwardly obeyed with my actions, but inwardly I was in rebellion against You. I repent for the lack of submission and honor in my heart. I repent for thinking that as long as I was obedient in my actions, my heart could think what it wanted. I realize today that I was only fooling myself. There is nothing hidden from Your eyes. I repent that I chose to worship the enemy with the thoughts and intent of my heart. I repent for worshiping a foreign god. I ask You to forgive me.*
>
> *I also say today that I refuse to give satan any place of affection in my heart. I confess anew that I choose You, Lord Jesus, as the king of my heart and my life. I bow my knee to the One True God and no one else. I will not allow any foreign god to sit in the seat of authority over my life. I will have no other*

gods beside You. I choose to worship You alone. Teach me how to approach Your altar and bring spiritual sacrifices that are pleasing and acceptable to You in Christ Jesus. I want to be a functioning part of Your royal priesthood. I submit myself—body, soul, and spirit—to You and You alone. In Jesus' name.

9

THE POWER OF SACRIFICE

As we've seen in the previous chapter, under the Old Covenant there were two types of sacrifices that were offered—atoning and non-atoning sacrifices. Atoning sacrifices were made as a payment for the penalty of sin, to cleanse the people from sin, and to restore their right standing with God (see Lev. 16). We no longer make these sacrifices as they were fulfilled in Jesus. He became the perfect sacrifice, once for all time. He paid the penalty for all sin for all time and made a way for us to become righteous in Him. His blood is the means by which all can be cleansed of sin and iniquity. There is no longer any need for the priests of God to offer sacrifices for sin. There is no spiritual sacrifice that you can bring for sin. Jesus was the sacrifice, and it was made once for all time!

The other type of sacrifice was the non-atoning sacrifice. These sacrifices had nothing to do with the remission of sin. They were brought to honor God and thank Him for His goodness and provision. These were freewill offerings that people brought because they just wanted to worship God and be in fellowship with Him. The sacrifices that we are to bring carry this non-atoning nature and should a sweet-smelling aroma for God. Previously, I explained how examples of these spiritual sacrifices are alluded to in the New Testament. But I believe that it would profit us to examine the non-atoning sacrifices of the Law to see what spiritual principles can be gleaned regarding these sacrifices. Again, these sacrifices were not for the remission of sins but were sacrifices brought to God to bring us close to Him, to bestow gifts upon Him, and to thank Him for His faithfulness and goodness.

THE WHOLE BURNT OFFERING: A LIVING SACRIFICE

> *I beseech you therefore, brethren, by the mercies of God, that you present your bodies a living sacrifice, holy, acceptable to God, which is your reasonable service* (Romans 12:1).

Here Paul is saying that our reasonable service as priests is to offer ourselves as a living sacrifice. The language is reminiscent of the whole burnt offering that was offered under the Old Covenant, so let us take a closer look at this type of offering.

Under the Old Covenant, a whole burnt offering was the commonest of offerings. It was offered every morning and evening on the altar and more frequently on holy days. It was to be a freewill offering, but the animal that was to be sacrificed had to be without blemish. There is much to be learned from studying the protocols of this offering, but I believe it is more important to note that the first mention of a burnt offering is before the Law was given. The burnt offering is first mentioned in Genesis 8:20-21:

> *Then Noah built an altar to the Lord, and took of every clean animal and of every clean bird, and offered burnt offerings on the altar. And the Lord smelled a soothing aroma. Then the Lord said in His heart, "I will never again curse the ground for man's sake, although the imagination of man's heart is evil from his youth; nor will I again destroy every living thing as I have done.*

When Noah is safely on land, the first thing that He does is bring an offering to the Lord. I believe that out of His love and gratitude to the Lord that he and his family survived the devastation of the flood, he brings a burnt offering. He takes clean animals and birds and offers them to the Lord. This is an extremely costly sacrifice. Remember, there are only a limited number of animals and birds that have survived, yet Noah takes this scarce commodity and offers it to the Lord. He burns them completely as an act of worship to God. This offering prompted a response from God. The Scripture says that the Lord smelled a sweet-smelling aroma and then He promised to never curse the ground again. Notice that it was the aroma of the offering that got God's attention. I believe that it was not the smell of the burning flesh but rather the aroma of Noah's heart of devotion that moved God to bless Noah. God then established covenant with him, not because Noah was without sin or perfect, but He established covenant based on Noah's burnt offering. The heart attitude of love and devotion that accompanied the sacrifice was what moved God to bless Noah.

The next mention of a burnt offering is with Abraham in Genesis 22:2:

> *Then He said, "Take now your son, your only son Isaac, whom you love, and go to the land of Moriah, and offer him there as a burnt offering on one of the mountains of which I shall tell you."*

Again, this is before the Law. God instructs Abraham to offer his son as a burnt offering. This is not about the remission of sin. This is about worshiping the Lord with your best, most costly sacrifice. It is about a heart so devoted to God that there is nothing you will refuse Him. It is about bringing a sacrifice in obedience with a willing heart. When Abraham does this, God provides a ram for the sacrifice. Abraham's willingness to bring a whole burnt offering served God's greater purposes for future generations. It provided the Israelites with a picture of a sacrificial animal dying in place of a man, thereby giving a veiled clue and legal precedent for the greater work of Jesus that would take place many years later.

From the above, we can see that the whole burnt offering, although widely used under the Law, carries significance apart from the law. It speaks about a total surrender of our own lives according to God's purposes. And it is to this type of total surrender that Paul is challenging the church in Romans 12:1. He is saying that becoming a whole, living sacrifice is our reasonable service of worship as priest of God. The daily laying down of our lives and our desires that He may have His way in us. The giving of our lives as a sacrifice to Him. Not that we die, but that we live. And we live, not for ourselves, but for Him.

As Paul says, this is our reasonable service. It is the base line. It is where we all start. This sacrifice is something that is required; we should not even be wondering whether we want to bring this sacrifice. It should be a natural first step. Unfortunately, in much of the church this is not so. Many are happy to give a few hours on a Sunday or perhaps a week or two in order to go on a missions trip. Others will give of their finances or abilities to help other believers, but this is *not* what Paul is talking about. He is talking about a *complete surrender* of our lives. A laying down of our own desires, dreams, and cares. A life that is set apart to fulfill God's purposes in every moment. A life that honors God's goodness and faithfulness to you. And you do not have to be in full-time ministry to do that! You simply have to be completely obedient to every word that God speaks to you and obey it from a heart of worship and honor. *This* is our reasonable service of worship.

This is one of the spiritual sacrifices that we, as priests, are to make every day. But how do we do that? Well, for me it is a simple prayer each morning. But I do it with intent, understanding that I am a priest bringing a sacrifice (myself) to God's altar. As I go to prayer, I am mindful that I am stepping onto God's trading floor and presenting myself as a living sacrifice. I am presenting the best offering I have—myself—from a place of thankfulness and honor toward the Lord for the blessing and favor He has bestowed on me, even when I do not deserve it. I am trading my plans, my times, my life for His plans and purposes for that day. That His will would be done in me and through me and not my own will. I am proclaiming that I love the Lord with all my heart, all my soul, and all my mind, thereby fulfilling the first and greatest commandment according to Jesus in Matthew 22:37.

My prayer would sound something like this:

> *Father, today I come before Your throne because of the blood and sacrifice of Jesus. I thank You that He became sin that I might obtain the righteousness of Christ. I thank You and honor You for Your love toward me and Your continued faithfulness toward me, even when I do not deserve it. Thank You for Jesus and His sacrifice, which enables me to present myself at Your altar, on Your trading floor. Today I lay down my life. I lay down my plans. I lay down my desires. I lay down all that I want out of today. I give myself as a living sacrifice. This is my reasonable service of worship to You. Let this sacrifice be holy and acceptable to You, I pray.*

The Power of Sacrifice

The prayer may be short, but I carry with me the conviction all day that I am not my own. My ear is turned to hear His voice that directs me. As soon as I hear Him instruct me, I do it without hesitation from a heart of worship. I am a living sacrifice. Now there will be days when He does not specifically instruct me to do anything differently. That does not mean I do nothing. *No!* I continue doing the work that is set before me with a submitted and thankful spirit. I complete my daily work with excellence and honor toward God. We are not crazy people who sit on our knees, only ever moving when they hear the voice of God. We are living sacrifices, prepared for every good work in Christ Jesus.

I want to emphasize here that being a living sacrifice is simply the start. As Paul says, it is our reasonable service of worship. That word reasonable is *logikós,* which means rational, reasonable, or what is logical to God (Strong's #G3050). If you look into the deeper meaning of this word, it explains that being a living sacrifice is God's "divine reasoning" in order to cause every decision in your life to have profound eternal meaning, even in earthly setbacks. This is why it should form the foundation of our service as priests. And I mean that—it is the foundation and not the entirety of our service! When we begin to talk about bringing sacrifices in church, many people tell me that as long as we are a living sacrifice, there is no need to bring any other sacrifices. Well, that is just not true! Just as the burnt offering was only one type of offering, there are also many other types of spiritual sacrifices that we need to bring as part of our priestly service.

It is interesting to note that under the Law, the burnt offering was placed on the altar and the grain and peace offerings were laid on top of the burnt offering. They were separate sweet-smelling offerings, but they were only offered once the burnt offering had been made, I believe that this is a wonderful picture for us as priests. Our foundational service of worship is the laying down of our lives for God's purposes—being the living sacrifice. Our other sacrifices are then layered over this living sacrifice. If this "layering" is the picture in the Old Covenant, it conveys an important spiritual principle to us. I would suspect that if we brought other sacrifices without first being a living sacrifice, they might not be acceptable to the Lord. (Just saying!)

Under the New Covenant, there is no instruction or law that says we have to bring sacrifices or offerings. Every offering is a freewill offering. That means that it is voluntary and brought because we want to bring it. No sacrifice should ever be made by force. Notice that Paul says in Romans 12:1, "*I beseech you therefore, brethren, by the mercies of God, that you present your bodies.*" Paul is not saying that we have to do it. He is beseeching us, which in plain English means that he is asking us urgently and fervently to do something. He is not commanding us; he is imploring us. No believer is forced to take up his role as a priest. In the same way, no believer is forced to bring spiritual sacrifices. But that does not mean that they are not real, integral components of our destiny in Christ. Each person can have as much or as little of their destiny in God as they want. We are a royal priesthood, but unless you take up your role as a priest and begin to bring spiritual sacrifices, you will never encounter that level of life in God. On that note, let's take a look at some of the other non-atoning sacrifices to see if we can draw any spiritual principles from them.

THE GRAIN OFFERING: RAISING A MEMORIAL

The grain offering was brought to worship God and acknowledge His provision. This offering was to be made from fine grain with oil and frankincense poured over it. It was an offering made by fire, but it was to be bloodless. The first thing we should note is that grain was probably very difficult to come by when the Israelites were in the wilderness. It was a desert; nothing grows there! If they had any grain, it was what they had brought with them and was being kept as seed to plant in the Promised Land. In order to bring a grain offering, it required the Israelites to give of something that was very rare and precious to them. They had to bring their seed (which was their future provision) as a sacrifice to God to honor Him as their provider! And remember, this was a freewill offering.

In addition, the grain had to be fine, which spoke of fine quality, but it also spoke of a very fine texture. That would require that the person spend time grinding the flour. If you have ever had to grind flour, you know that it is a very physically intensive and time-consuming task. And remember that the Israelites did not have electric grinding machines. This sacrifice was something that required hours of hard labor on the part of the offerer in order to have fine grain to sacrifice.

The oil and the frankincense were also scarce, expensive ingredients. This sacrifice was costly on many levels. The offering could be presented in many different forms—cooked, baked, or raw. God did not prescribe its form, but it was not allowed to have any leaven or honey in it. Decomposition or decaying happens in the leavening process and honey hastens this process. In Scripture, leaven often symbolizes sin and wickedness. God is being clear that no sin or death should be a part of this sacrifice. I believe this points again to our heart attitudes when bringing such a sacrifice.

When the priests offered this sacrifice on the altar, they only placed a handful in the fire. This was known as the memorial offering. The balance of the sacrifice was given to the priests to live on. This is why this type of sacrifice or offering is sometimes called a memorial offering. At times in our lives, it is helpful to bring a "grain offering" before the Lord as a memorial offering. This is a sacrifice that you bring that is very costly to you and is provided through some hard work of your own. This sacrifice is the fruit of your labor that you want to give as a gift to the Lord to thank Him for His faithfulness and provision in your life. When you bring it, you may even be taking the seed of your next season to give it to Him as a sacrifice on His trading floor. And you are doing it with great honor and love in your heart. There is not a hint of anger, manipulation, or frustration in your sacrifice. You freely bring this sacrifice because you know that it is God who has blessed you with the ability to produce it in the first place. When it is offered from this heart, the sacrifice will be accepted by God and burnt up in His fire; a pleasing aroma will come up to Him. The testimony of your sacrifice will be as a memorial before His throne that speaks continually of His faithfulness to you. Think about it—God will have a constant reminder of you and your thankfulness toward Him. You will have His attention! His eyes will be turned toward you so that He might strongly support you because your heart is loyal toward Him (see 2 Chron. 16:9).

I believe that this is a picture of the spiritual sacrifice that the church in Philippi brought when they gave an offering to Paul. They gave an offering that was costly to them. Scripture does not say exactly what it was, but we know it sustained Paul so it had to have been material resources. It was the fruit of their labor that they gave to Paul, but it was a spiritual offering to the Lord. The physical offering went to Paul, but the spiritual sacrifice of the church ascended as a sweet-smelling savor to the Lord. Paul confirmed this fact when he said that it was "a sweet-smelling aroma, an acceptable sacrifice, well pleasing to God" (Phil. 4:18). And Paul also told us what the result of this spiritual sacrifice would be in Philippians 4:17:

> *Not that I seek the gift, but I seek the fruit that abounds to your account.*

He was saying that he longed for the churches to understand that it was important to bring this type of spiritual sacrifice, not because he wanted the gifts but because he understood that when they brought this spiritual sacrifice onto God's trading floor, they received abundant fruit back in the work that they were doing. Remember, this sacrifice is taken from the fruit of your labor. When you step onto God's trading floor and give it as a sacrifice to Him, it releases "fruit that abounds to your account." You gave of the fruit of your labor, but more fruit is about to be released to you. You are experiencing increase through trading!

THE PEACE OFFERING

This is a voluntary offering that is brought in thanksgiving to God because He is the One who completes us and gives us peace. This sacrifice was layered on the other two offerings. Only once those were in place could the peace of this offering be established. In this offering, an animal without blemish is brought for sacrifice, but what distinguishes this offering is that all three parties to the sacrifice eat of the sacrifice. This speaks about a meal that is shared between all. The blood and the fat of the sacrifice is offered on the altar, the breast and shoulder are given to the priest, and the offerer receives the rest of the animal for him and his family to feast upon. This sacrifice pictures God the Father, Jesus the High Priest, and us, His people, seated at a table enjoying a meal in peace with one another. Sounds rather like the communion table to me. Jesus is our peace offering, and because of His sacrifice He mediated a place of peace between God and mankind.

This type of spiritual offering is brought when we, as priests, bring offerings that facilitate peace between God and man. This means that we make sacrifices in our lives so that others may be blessed and glimpse the love and passion of God's heart for them. I believe that this is the type of spiritual sacrifice that Paul was referring to in Hebrews 13:15-16:

> *Therefore by Him let us continually offer the sacrifice of praise to God, that is, the fruit of*

our lips, giving thanks to His name. But do not forget to do good and to share, for with such sacrifices God is well pleased.

Paul is instructing the church to continually offer the spiritual sacrifice of thanksgiving and praise, but we must remember that there are other sacrifices as well. And he points out that these are the sacrifices that are well-pleasing to God. In other words, these sacrifices release a sweet-smelling savor to the Lord. We see that the sacrifice of praise is the speaking out of thanksgiving, but what are these other sacrifices? Paul says that we should not forget to "do good." That word *good* in the original Greek means "well-doing or beneficence" (Strong's #G2140). The good that we should do is to be directed toward others and not ourselves. As New Covenant priests, we have a responsibility to make sacrifices that will benefit others. We do not only bring offerings that would cause God to look upon and respond to us, but we bring sacrifices that are purely for the benefit of others.

The word for "share" in this Scripture is *koinōnía* (Strong's #G2842). Now, this word can be interpreted in three ways according to Strong's Concordance. It can mean fellowship or participation in community, but in our Scripture it means "a gift jointly contributed or a contribution as exhibiting an embodiment and proof of fellowship." When Paul exhorts the church to do good and share, he is saying that we should make sacrificial offerings to others that would cause them to benefit and experience the love and peace of God in their lives. We see this word *koinōnía* is also used to indicate a "contribution" in Second Corinthians 8:3-4:

> *For I bear witness that according to their ability, yes, and beyond their ability, they were freely willing, imploring us with much urgency that we would receive the gift and the fellowship of the ministering to the saints.*

Paul is commending the churches in Macedonia for their extravagant giving to the poor believers in Jerusalem. Notice that it was a *freewill* offering—they were not forced to give anything. In fact it seems that Paul was taken by surprise with their insistence to give an offering. The Macedonians were experiencing intense trials of their own, but despite that they gave out of the little they had so that others who were struggling should experience the provision and love of God. What a wonderful example of a spiritual sacrifice. But I want you to notice what he says next:

> *And not only as we had hoped, but they first gave themselves to the Lord, and then to us by the will of God* (2 Corinthians 8:5).

This tells us that the Macedonian church understood that being a "living sacrifice" was the beginning. They "layered" their spiritual sacrifices upon this first whole burnt offering to the Lord!

There can be no trading without sacrifice. A sacrifice is an extremely powerful act. It is something that we do in the natural that releases the supernatural realm to intervene and change the course of natural events. Sacrifice demands a response from the spirit realm, and this is why I say that sacrifice triggers trading.

SACRIFICE TRIGGERS TRADING

The reason that God has called us to be a royal priesthood and to bring these spiritual sacrifices in the True Tabernacle is so that we can trade with Him. Each time we bring a sacrifice, we are positioned on the trading floor and our sacrifice releases a sweet-smelling aroma that draws His attention. The sacrifice indicates our readiness and desire to trade with Him. It tells Him that we are His special people and we understand our role as stewards who are to bring increase through trading. It tells Him we are ready to trade with Him. This is why, once we have brought our sacrifice, we should linger on the trading floor and listen for His voice. The spiritual sacrifice was a declaration of our understanding and intent to trade. If we step off the trading floor and continue with life, we miss hearing Him speak. We miss hearing Him share His heart with us. We miss our opportunity to trade. Once we have brought our sacrifice and it has been accepted, it is right that we wait to hear what God would share with us. For it is in this place that He will share something of His heart. Let me give a practical example so you can see how this would look in the natural.

When believers gather to worship, if they truly intend to worship they will start by presenting themselves as a living sacrifice. This means that before they come to the service, they will lay down all their personal agendas for the meeting. Corporate meetings are not the place to bring your list of wants and needs to God anyway. That should be done in your personal prayer times. When we come to corporate worship services, we come to bring a sacrifice of praise and thanksgiving to the Lord.

Remember, worship is all about sacrifice. We start by sacrificing all our own desires and laying our lives down as a living sacrifice. We want this time to be all about God and what *He* wants. When we gather with this in mind, we become a corporate living sacrifice, and the sweet-smelling savor of this sacrifice rapidly catches God's attention. This is why, when you participate in these types of meetings, as soon as you start you are able to ascend the hill of the Lord, step before His throne, and you will always see a trading floor open in this place.

In this place of corporate worship, you may want bring an offering that is simply to say how much you love God. You may want to bring an offering to thank Him for His faithfulness and goodness to you. The grain offering is our picture for this—an offering from the fruit of our labors. This is why we bring financial offerings as a part of our worship. Finances are the fruit of our labors. We work all week to receive a financial payment for our time and skills. Money is the fruit of our labors. And when we are on the trading floor, we want to bring this offering in worship and honor to the Lord. We are "layering" another offering on top of our burnt offering.

All of this sacrifice is creating an increasing incense and aroma before the Lord. He is coming close to us. Now is the time that we should be open to hearing His voice. He is coming close to be with us and share with us what is on His heart. In a worship service, this might look like a prophetic word coming forth. It might be the Word being preached. Or it might be a testimony being shared. However the service proceeds, we now need to be aware that our worship has positioned us to trade with God. He *will* speak, and it will be an opportunity to trade with Him.

When God speaks, He is releasing a word out of Heaven, which is a seed. That seed carries the potential of a Kingdom reality within it. God is declaring something that He wants to see established in the earth, but it is still in seed form. He is looking for good soil for this seed. He wants it to land in the heart of a person who will hear and understand or receive the word so that it can bear a harvest in due season. He does not want it land on the wayside and be taken by the enemy. He does not want it to be lost or unfruitful because the soil is rocky or filled with thorns. (Of course, I am referring to the parable of the sower in Matthew 13:18-23.) God wants the word of the Kingdom to be established and bear much fruit! That means that in the preaching, the prophetic word, or the testimony, there is Kingdom seed being released from Heaven. As a good steward, we want to present the soil of our hearts as a landing place for this seed. We want to volunteer our hearts. How do we do that?

Well, the definition of the word *volunteer* means "a person who freely offers to do something." Did you see that—freely offers. I believe that the appropriate way to volunteer our hearts is to *freely offer* to the Lord. A freewill offering will say to the Lord, "I hear what is on Your heart; I want to partner with You! *Pick me, pick me!* I want to receive Your Kingdom seed. I have an ear to hear what You are saying and a heart that understands Your ways. I choose to walk in them to see a harvest come from this seed. *Pick me!*" This is good ground and it *will* receive the seed of the Kingdom. When God releases His Kingdom seed during a service, it is right and appropriate, if your heart is stirred, to bring a freewill offering that volunteers your heart to receive that seed. You are not forced to bring your offering; you choose to bring it. You are bringing your seed as a freewill offering in order to receive His seed. It is not a manipulation; it a faithful steward trading what he has in order to bring increase to the Kingdom.

We see this illustrated in Exodus 35:4-29. When Moses is getting ready to build the tabernacle, he tells the people that whoever has a willing heart and wants to bring an offering to the Lord should do so in order for the tabernacle can be built. And verse 21 confirms, *"Then everyone came whose heart was stirred, and everyone whose spirit was willing, and they brought the Lord's offering for the work of the tabernacle of meeting, for all its service, and for the holy garments."* God gave Moses an instruction to build the tabernacle, but He also instructed Moses to offer the people an opportunity to be a part of the building of it. God did not force anyone to be a part of it. He only wanted those who had a *willing* heart and wanted to bring an offering. God wants us to be a part of what He is establishing in the earth, but He is looking for willing participants. He only receives from those whose hearts are stirred and whose spirits are willing!

This is just one example of how our sacrifices position us on the trading floor of Heaven and empower us to trade with God to see the Kingdom come on earth as it is in Heaven.

THE POWER OF SACRIFICE TO DELIVER A NATION

Sacrifice and trading have the power to deliver a nation from the stranglehold of corruption and compromise. Malachi 3:3-5 explains that there is an offering or sacrifice that causes the Lord to come near us for judgement:

> *He will sit as a refiner and a purifier of silver; He will purify the sons of Levi, and purge them as gold and silver, that they may offer to the Lord an offering in righteousness.*
>
> *"Then the offering of Judah and Jerusalem will be pleasant to the Lord, as in the days of old, as in former years. And I will come near you for judgment; I will be a swift witness against sorcerers, against adulterers, against perjurers, against those who exploit wage earners and widows and orphans, and against those who turn away an alien—because they do not fear Me," says the Lord of hosts.*

The book of Malachi was written during a time when Israel was deeply in sin. It was less than 100 years after returning from the captivity, and the nation had already exceeded its former iniquities, which brought on the Babylonian deportations. The anticipated Messiah had still not come, and Israel's future was looking hopeless. The people and the priests did what was good in their own eyes, yet they brought their sacrifices at the temple thinking that the outward ritual would maintain their relationship with God. Everyone was doing their religious duty, but their hearts and lives were far from God. It is into this situation that Malachi stepped and began to rebuke the priests and the people for their corruption and wickedness.

He explained in Malachi 2 that the Lord's coming, which they were seeking, would be in judgment to refine, purify, and purge. He would deal with the priests, and then they would again bring offerings that would please Him. I believe that this is applicable today. God is speaking to His royal priesthood. He is seeking to refine us and purge us from our wicked ways. He is calling us out of ritualized, powerless religion and cleansing us from generational iniquities. Once He has completed this process in us, He will teach us how to bring offerings in righteousness. We will understand how to bring sacrifices from a heart of worship that rise as a sweet-smelling aroma to Him. And then, He will come near for judgement.

The Scripture says that when the offering of Judah and Jerusalem is pleasant as in the days of old, then He will come near for judgement. He will begin to deal those whose wickedness defiles a nation. He will deal with His enemies and those who oppress His people. Notice that God will come near to judge them. Our part is to bring the offering in righteousness. If we want to see our nations delivered from the systems of social injustice, we must learn to bring offerings in righteousness!

Sacrifice triggers trading, and without trading we will not redeem what has been stolen from us or restore the Kingdom that wants to come. It is therefore imperative that we learn how to intentionally bring our spiritual sacrifices before the Lord in such a way that they are pleasing to Him.

SACRIFICES MUST BE ACCEPTABLE TO GOD

Peter reminds us in First Peter 2:5 that our sacrifices are to be *"acceptable to God* through Jesus Christ." Sacrifices need to be accepted. This is something that is often overlooked in Christianity. We think that we can bring whatever sacrifice we would like in whatever manner we like and that God will be happy with it. This is just not true. Just think about the offering that was taken up at the last service you attended. Your offerings were meant to be a sacrifice to the Lord. You probably had a time when everyone placed their offering in the basket and then the pastor or one of the leaders prayed over it, but did anyone wait to see whether God accepted the offering? Was He pleased with the sacrifice? Was it a sweet-smelling aroma to Him? Did it draw His attention to you as a congregation? What is the witness of your sacrifice before the Lord? Just asking! We must realize that there are offerings and sacrifices that God does not accept.

SACRIFICES CANNOT REPLACE OBEDIENCE

God does not accept a sacrifice given in place of obedience. There are times when God tells us to do something and we do not do it. Sometimes we forget to do it, but sometimes we decide that we do not really want to do it. Then when we are in His presence again, we are reminded about it and feel a little guilty, so we give some extra money in the offering. Or we go and serve at the feeding project to ease our conscience. Your sacrifice, whether it was the money or the service, will not be acceptable to God. You are wasting your time and money. It will be rejected and not bear any fruit for the Kingdom. Why? Because sacrifice is not a substitute for obedience! God told this to Saul when he tried to justify his disobedience in First Samuel 15:22:

> *Has the Lord as great delight in burnt offerings and sacrifices, as in obeying the voice of the Lord? Behold, to obey is better than sacrifice, and to heed than the fat of rams.*

God would not accept the sacrifices that the people were bringing to Him because He had instructed them to kill everything. They disobeyed God and then tried to cover their disobedience by bringing offerings. In the same way, God will not accept your spiritual sacrifice if you have not been obedient to obey His word to you. God wants obedience more than sacrifice, but that does not mean that He does not want us to bring sacrifices at all. He simply will not let us use sacrifices in place of obedience!

YOU CANNOT MANIPULATE GOD WITH YOUR SACRIFICE

Your heart motive is the voice of your sacrifice when you trade. We have spoken at length about how the attitude of your heart is of vital importance when stepping onto the trading floor. But I want you to realize that a wrong heart motive will cause your sacrifice to be unacceptable to the Lord. If your heart has an ulterior motive in bringing your sacrifice or if you are in any way reluctant to bring this sacrifice, it will be rejected. This is what happened to Cain in Genesis 4:3-5:

> *And in the process of time it came to pass that Cain brought an offering of the fruit of the ground to the Lord. Abel also brought of the firstborn of his flock and of their fat. And the Lord respected Abel and his offering, but He did not respect Cain and his offering. And Cain was very angry, and his countenance fell.*

At a certain time, both of these men brought an offering to the Lord. God accepted one, and the other He rejected. What was the difference in these offerings that caused God to reject one and accept another? Cain brought an offering of the fruit of the ground. Abel brought the firstborn of his flock, and he brought the fat portions as his sacrifice. Abel brought the first and the best of what he had. This speaks of a heart attitude that is looking for the very best way that he could honor the Lord and worship Him with his sacrifice. And he succeeded. Hebrews 11:4 tells us:

> *By faith Abel offered to God a more excellent sacrifice than Cain, through which he obtained witness that he was righteous, God testifying of his gifts; and through it he being dead still speaks.*

Abel's offering was received by God and its voice still witnesses in the realm of Heaven today. Cain's offering was very different. Scripture says that he simply brought "an offering." This tells us that Cain knew he had to bring an offering, so he took some of the fruit of the ground and brought it. He did not look to bring anything special. He did not look for a way to honor God. He did this out of duty and not out of a heart of worship. This caused his sacrifice to be rejected.

God will not be manipulated. You cannot bring offerings out of duty to keep Him happy. You sacrifice *will* be rejected. If you are putting money in that offering plate every Sunday because you *have* to—your offering is being rejected. If you are serving in the children's church to earn points with God—your sacrifice is being rejected. When you bring a sacrifice, it must come from a heart of love and worship for God. If your heart is not in that place, do not bring your sacrifice *yet*. Get your heart sorted out. Deal with your anger, unforgiveness, frustration, or whatever it is, and then bring your sacrifice. Do not be like Cain, who refused to deal with his heart, got offended, and chose to stop worshiping God altogether.

Our hearts' testimony is the voice attached to our sacrifice. If it does not sound like worship, it will not be an acceptable sacrifice.

SACRIFICES SHOULD BE COSTLY

All sacrifices are not equal. Jesus' sacrifice of His life is not equal to a person who sacrifices chocolate for Lent. Both are a sacrifice. Both people are laying down something that has value to them and it is something that they would prefer to retain. Both of them are making their sacrifice out of love for God and as a sign of their submission to Him. But these sacrifices will have vastly different effects on the natural world. Why? One sacrifice had greater power than the other. Why? One cost the giver more than the other. When we talk about sacrifices and the power of sacrifices, we need to understand that the cost of the sacrifice is important!

The greater the sacrifice, the greater the response from the spirit realm. This is clearly seen when we consider the trading done on demonic trading floors. When people intentionally trade with satan for something, he prescribes the type of sacrifice that they should bring to him. The type of sacrifice is dependent on what they expect to receive in the trade. If they want power over another individual, perhaps they have to bring a sacrifice of an animal. But if they want power to win a war over a neighboring tribe, the sacrifice would probably have to be another person's life. To influence a person will require the release of a certain amount of power from the demonic realm. The measure of power that needs to be released in order to give victory over a whole tribe is exponentially greater. Therefore, the sacrifice needs to be exponentially greater. This principle holds true throughout the spiritual realm and explains why giving up chocolate for forty days will not afford the same result as Jesus laying His life down.

David understood this principle. When he sinned against God by numbering the people in First Chronicles 21:1-7, he brought a judgment of God on the whole nation. In order to remove the iniquity, God gave him a choice of three "punishments." We see that he chose the third option in First Chronicles 21:12:

> *For three days the sword of the Lord—the plague in the land, with the angel of the Lord destroying throughout all the territory of Israel.*

David entrusted himself to the hands of the Lord rather than the hand of man because he knew that God's mercies were great. He knew that God would want to show mercy to His people, and I believe that David chose this option so that he could continue to cry out to the Lord and perhaps have Him stop or shorten the plague. And this is what happened:

> *So the Lord sent a plague upon Israel, and seventy thousand men of Israel fell. And God sent an angel to Jerusalem to destroy it. As he was destroying, the Lord looked and relented of the disaster, and said to the angel who was destroying, "It is enough; now restrain your hand." And the angel of the Lord stood by the threshing floor of Ornan the Jebusite* (1 Chronicles 21:14-15).

God wanted to have mercy on Jerusalem. He restrained the hand of the angel, but his sword was still drawn. David, the one with a heart after God, understood that God wanted to show mercy and so he presented himself as a living sacrifice. His heart of love for God and the people caused him to ask God to bring the plague on him and his house and not the people. David was willing to sacrifice his own life for the sake of God's people. He laid down his life, his desires, and his dreams in order that God would have His desire. As that sacrifice came before the Lord, I believe that he remembered David and Israel and all that He loved about His special people, and He had mercy on them and gave David another way in which to redeem the situation.

God instructed David to build an altar on the threshing floor of Ornan. When David went to the floor, Ornan offered to give it to him for free, together with all the oxen, the threshing implements, and the grain necessary to bring the offerings. I sometimes think that if that was me, I would have rejoiced at "God's provision" in the situation. But David knew God. His response is legendary and displays his understanding of the power of sacrifice. First Chronicles 21:24 tells us:

> *Then King David said to Ornan, "No, but I will surely buy it for the full price, for I will not take what is yours for the Lord, nor offer burnt offerings with that which costs me nothing."*

The plague was released due to David's sin, but God in His great mercy had stayed the hand of the angel as he was about to destroy Jerusalem. I think that David was overwhelmed by the goodness and faithfulness of God. God was choosing to save the nation from a punishment that should rightfully have been released. David wanted to worship God extravagantly. He wanted God to know how much he loved Him. He wanted this sacrifice to bless God that He would not be able to stay away from Jerusalem. David knew that this sacrifice would save the nation and many lives. If God had not had mercy on him and Israel, they would have been destroyed. His thankfulness and gratitude to God was enormous. This sacrifice would convey what was in his heart. This could not be any old sacrifice. This could not cost him nothing. This sacrifice was his worship. It had to be the best sacrifice that he could bring.

We know that David paid 600 shekels of gold by weight for the place, built the altar, and made burnt and peace offerings on it. God accepted his sacrifice when *"He answered him from*

Heaven by fire on the altar of burnt offering" (1 Chron. 21:26). David's sacrifice was acceptable. And this natural act created a supernatural response from Heaven, which in turn changed the natural world.

> *So the Lord commanded the angel, and he returned his sword to its sheath* (1 Chronicles 21:27).

The plague was stopped; Jerusalem was saved and the people in it. That is the power of a sacrifice!

ACCEPTABLE SACRIFICES PROVOKE A RESPONSE FROM HEAVEN

> *So Cornelius said, "Four days ago I was fasting until this hour; and at the ninth hour I prayed in my house, and behold, a man stood before me in bright clothing, and said, 'Cornelius, your prayer has been heard, and your alms are remembered in the sight of God. Send therefore to Joppa and call Simon here, whose surname is Peter. He is lodging in the house of Simon, a tanner, by the sea. When he comes, he will speak to you.' So I sent to you immediately, and you have done well to come. Now therefore, we are all present before God, to hear all the things commanded you by God"* (Acts 10:30-33).

Cornelius was a Gentile, but Acts 10:2 says that he was *"a devout man and one who feared God with all his household, who gave alms generously to the people, and prayed to God always."* Even though he was not schooled in the Jewish system of sacrifices, he knew how to bring spiritual sacrifices. He fasted and prayed. He lived righteously and taught his household to do the same. He chose to serve and fear God in faith. He gave to the poor generously. This man knew how to bring sacrifices that were accepted by God. His sacrifices carried his heart of devotion and created a memorial before the Lord that captured God's attention. But more than that, his sacrifices provoked God to respond to him. God sent an angel and then He sent Peter to bring the gospel of salvation to this household. One man's acceptable sacrifice caused God to release the message of salvation to the world from his house. A natural act made from a heart of worship provoked an immensely significant response from Heaven that forever changed the natural world. God cannot resist the aroma of a sweet-smelling sacrifice. It will always get His attention and cause Him to respond to bring change to the world around us.

THE DYNAMICS OF TRADING

by Robert Henderson

WHEN WE TALK FUNCTIONALLY ABOUT TRADING, WE can see it in the ministry of Jesus. Jesus stepped onto the trading floors of Heaven frequently in His ministry. He understood this dimension. In fact, this was one of the realms He functioned in to perform His miracles. However, in these miracles from the trading floors of Heaven, we can see principles we too are to function in. In the miracles are contained secrets to seeing things shift in the natural. For instance, trading was involved in the turning of the water into wine.

In John 2:1-11, we see the miracle at the wedding of Cana of Galilee. The Bible calls this the first miracle of Jesus at least in this region.

> *On the third day there was a wedding in Cana of Galilee, and the mother of Jesus was there. Now both Jesus and His disciples were invited to the wedding.* And when they ran out of wine, the mother of Jesus said to Him, "They have no wine."
>
> *Jesus said to her, "Woman, what does your concern have to do with Me? My hour has not yet come."*
>
> *His mother said to the servants, "Whatever He says to you, do it."*
>
> *Now there were set there six waterpots of stone, according to the manner of purification of the Jews, containing twenty or thirty gallons apiece. Jesus said to them, "Fill the waterpots with water." And they filled them up to the brim. And He said to them, "Draw some out now, and take it to the master of the feast." And they took it. When the master of the feast had tasted the water that was made wine, and did not know where it came from* (but the servants who had drawn the water knew), *the master of the feast called the bridegroom. And he said to him, "Every man at the beginning sets out the good wine, and when the guests have well drunk,*

then the inferior. You have kept the good wine until now!"

This beginning of signs Jesus did in Cana of Galilee, and manifested His glory; and His disciples believed in Him.

Jesus' mother, Mary, desires Him to help with the situation of the wine running out in the wedding feast. The Bible doesn't say why she desires Him to involve Himself. Some have said it is because she is looking for validation. Mary until this time is thought to be an unclean woman who cheated on Joseph before their official marriage. She wants Jesus not only to display who she knows Him to be but also to silence all those who consider her impure and a woman worthy of death. She is looked upon as one guilty of fornication and adultery because she ended up pregnant before marriage. The law demands for such a one to be stoned to death. Joseph had saved her from this end because he cared so much for her. An angel had then appeared to him in a dream and told him the real facts of the story. As a result, Mary and Joseph are both looked upon with doubt, ridicule, and even contempt. If Jesus would just begin to show His power publicly as the Son of God, these years of disgrace could be ended. As a result, Mary is asking Jesus to please supernaturally deal with this problem of there being no wine.

At first, Jesus seems to resist. He tells Mary that the problem is not His problem. Mary then tells the servants to do whatever Jesus tells them to do. The undistracted obedience of the servants seems to change Jesus' attitude about the matter. When the servants are committed to absolute obedience, Jesus steps into the situation. This shows that obedience and surrender grasp the heart of God. When there are people who are willing to obey absolutely, God is prepared to move. The power of surrender and obedience will always move the heart of God to act. May we be that people of obedience who move the heart of God and cause His power to be seen.

Jesus then tells the servants to fill up the water pots. There are six water pots that hold 20 to 30 gallons apiece. These are huge vessels. This means their combined capacity is 120 to 180 gallons of liquid. To fill these water pots is a major ordeal. There is no running water. To fill the pots will require drawing water from a well, up to 180 gallons of it. This is major work. Yet the servants do as Jesus commanded. Their obedience is absolutely complete. Jesus then commands them to draw the water and give it to the master of the feast. Whereas filling the water pots was just hard work, presenting this water is a step of faith. They are moving now into the faith realm. As they do, the supernatural happens. Somewhere in this process, the miracle occurs. The water becomes wine. It is such good wine that the master of the feast comments on the excellence of it. He declares, "The best has been saved until last." But how did this miracle really occur?

It happened because a trade was made. The servants took that which was natural, their effort, and exchanged it in the spirit realm. When they chose to obey Jesus, they stepped with Jesus onto the trading floors of Heaven. They stepped into the spirit world and traded their natural efforts for something supernatural. They also by faith presented the water to the master of the feast as wine. Hard work and faith became a trade in the spirit realm. The result was water becoming wine. They traded what they had in the natural realm to produce something supernatural. This is also how we make our trades.

We live in a natural world. We can, however, take what is natural and trade it to produce the supernatural. The issue is, will we trade our labors and faith to see the supernatural of God manifested? We can take our labors or what our labors produce, which is money, and by faith present them on the trading floor of the spirit. This is what the servants did when they explicitly obeyed Jesus. They traded in the spirit and faith realm and moved into the supernatural. When Jesus asks us to obey, He is inviting us onto the trading floors of Heaven. He is granting us an opportunity to partake with Him in the glories of the Kingdom of God and its function.

One of the amazing things in this first miracle is that it appears no one really knew the backstory except the servants. Yet everyone at the party received the benefits of Jesus' miracle-working power and the servants' obedience. Even the disciples of Jesus were only spectators to this miracle, but the whole community received the blessing of the servants' obedience without knowing what they had done. This paints a picture of how God does things at times. No miracle just happens. Somebody paid the price to see it occur. Somebody traded on the trading floors of Heaven. They traded through obedience to the Lord. They traded through hours of prayer, travail, and intercession. They traded through giving financially in faith. They traded through investing that which was precious. As they did this, they secured a supernatural breakthrough—not just for themselves, but for a community and even a culture.

In these times, we are aware that God wants to change cultures to reflect His Kingdom. We are not talking about making nations religious states. We are talking about nations developing a Kingdom culture consistent with Judeo-Christian values. This can happen through "the servants" trading. As the church, God's ekklesia, begins to step onto the trading floor of Heaven, we can secure blessings for whole nations. What we as God's people/servants do in the secret places of the trading floors can shift the culture of nations. No one will know what we have done. Only Heaven will applaud us. The politicians will take the credit. Heaven, however, will record our trading that allowed God to reclaim nations back to His purpose and destiny for them.

To really understand this, let's look at Malachi 3:2-5.

> *But who can endure the day of His coming? And who can stand when He appears? For He is like a refiner's fire and like launderers' soap. He will sit as a refiner and a purifier of silver; He will purify the sons of Levi, and purge them as gold and silver, that they may offer to the Lord an offering in righteousness.*
>
> *"Then the offering of Judah and Jerusalem will be pleasant to the Lord, as in the days of old, as in former years. And I will come near you for judgment; I will be a swift witness against sorcerers, against adulterers, against perjurers, against those who exploit wage earners and widows and orphans, and against those who*

> *turn away an alien—because they do not fear Me," says the Lord of hosts.*

We see that an offering in righteousness allows judgments against all that afflicts society. Notice that God purifies those who bring offerings to Him. This allows them to present offerings that are accepted and acknowledged before God. This in turn renders judgments or verdicts against wickedness and evil in society. Adultery, perjury, economic oppression, sorcery, and others are all judged. God Himself is a swift witness against these things that defile and pollute a nation and its culture. This can all happen because money, finances, and offerings have a voice and give a testimony. Hebrews 7:8 clearly states that the tithe gives a witness or testimony in Heaven.

> *Here mortal men receive tithes, but there he receives them, of whom it is witnessed that he lives.*

The tithe makes a judicial statement in Heaven that the tither believes He lives. Jesus, as our High Priest after the order of Melchizedek, is alive and functioning on our behalf. We don't give our tithe to something that is dead. We present our tithe to One who is alive and presiding over a living priesthood on our behalf. We connect to this priesthood through our tithe just as Abraham did in his day. We are of the seed of Abraham and therefore have his nature in us. What Abraham's faith propelled him to do, we are propelled to do as well. Abraham was an Old Testament man who lived from New Testament revelation. He lived outside his time by the revelation he had. We too live outside our time by the revelation we carry. The limits on others are not on us as we by faith enter the fullness of all Jesus died for us to have and His priesthood brings us into. The tithe we bring connects us to this priesthood and gives testimony in the Courts of Heaven. Our money speaks. It is our testimony that Jesus is alive. Another Scripture that shows money speaks is James 5:4. This verse says the money that was held back and not given to whom it rightfully belongs is crying out.

> *Indeed the wages of the laborers who mowed your fields, which you kept back by fraud, cry out; and the cries of the reapers have reached the ears of the Lord of Sabaoth.*

This money is crying out for judgment on those who are economically oppressing laborers. I believe that adjustments to economic systems can occur because money is crying out when it isn't in the right hands. Money is crying out to be moved to the hands it is supposed to be in. Whether this is money owed to those who have worked for it or it belongs to someone by inheritance, money is speaking and crying out to come to its rightful owner. We should agree with the testimony and voice of that money that is rightfully ours. Money has a voice and is releasing a testimony before the Lord, giving Him the right to render judgments.

When Malachi declared that God would be a swift witness and render judgments because of offerings of righteousness it was with this understanding. The money brought in an offering was releasing a testimony. To really grasp this, we need to recognize the dynamics that happen with an offering in righteousness. We bring our offering before the trading floors of Heaven, which is the fiery stone (see Ezek. 28:14-16). As we present our offerings in righteousness on the fiery stones, the fire of God consumes our offering in the spirit. This in turn releases a smoke or incense before the Lord. That aroma/smoke/incense creates a testimony before the Lord that can move His heart. This is what happened in the days of Noah in Genesis 8:20-22.

> *Then Noah built an altar to the Lord, and took of every clean animal and of every clean bird, and offered burnt offerings on the altar. And the Lord smelled a soothing aroma. Then the Lord said in His heart, "I will never again curse the ground for man's sake, although the imagination of man's heart is evil from his youth; nor will I again destroy every living thing as I have done.*
>
> *"While the earth remains, seedtime and harvest, cold and heat, winter and summer, and day and night shall not cease."*

As Noah came out of the ark, he offered burnt offerings to the Lord. He was in essence stepping onto the fiery stones in the spirit realm. He presented a pleasing offering to God. As God smelled the aroma of Noah's sacrifice, which was not the stench of burning flesh but the aroma of Noah's heart, God's heart was moved. He released a judicial decree that the earth would no longer labor under a curse. It would now be free to function under the blessings and procedure of the Lord. This happened because Noah offered an acceptable sacrifice on an earthly altar, but it was received on the fiery stones of the heavenly altar. The transaction he made with God in the spirit realm allowed God to set the earth free from its curse. God is looking for those who will trade with Him. He is searching for those who will come before Him as kingly priests and offer spiritual sacrifices. First Peter 2:5 declares that we as kingly priests are here to function in this capacity.

> *You also, as living stones, are being built up a spiritual house, a holy priesthood, to offer up spiritual sacrifices acceptable to God through Jesus Christ.*

Through spiritual sacrifice in the heavenly dimension we shift things for God's passion and will to be done in the earth. What a glorious privilege and honor we have been given. We can step onto the trading floors of Heaven and offer even financial offerings that carry great spiritual significance. We can trade for our destinies, the destinies of our families, and even the destinies of nations.

Another place in Scripture we can see a trade being made that produced miraculous results is John 6:5-14.

> *Then Jesus lifted up His eyes, and seeing a great multitude coming toward Him, He said to Philip, "Where shall we buy bread, that these may eat?" But this He said to test him, for He Himself knew what He would do.*

> *Philip answered Him, "Two hundred denarii worth of bread is not sufficient for them, that every one of them may have a little."*
>
> *One of His disciples, Andrew, Simon Peter's brother, said to Him, "There is a lad here who has five barley loaves and two small fish, but what are they among so many?"*
>
> *Then Jesus said, "Make the people sit down." Now there was much grass in the place. So the men sat down, in number about five thousand. And Jesus took the loaves, and when He had given thanks He distributed them to the disciples, and the disciples to those sitting down; and likewise of the fish, as much as they wanted. So when they were filled, He said to His disciples, "Gather up the fragments that remain, so that nothing is lost." Therefore they gathered them up, and filled twelve baskets with the fragments of the five barley loaves which were left over by those who had eaten. Then those men, when they had seen the sign that Jesus did, said, "This is truly the Prophet who is to come into the world."*

Jesus desires to feed the thousands, but there is nothing available, it seems, to do it with. He is asking His disciples how they are going to be able to accomplish this. For just an instant, Andrew gets a glimpse into the spirit realm that Jesus is functioning in. He declares that there is a boy with five loaves and two fishes that could be used. Then his logic and intellect override this moment of faith and he declares, "But what are they among so many?"

This happens to us many times as we are learning to step into the spiritual realm through faith. We get glimpses and impulses from the Spirit but then dismiss them with our natural mind. We must learn to discern these as from the Lord and embrace them. From these encounters, we can see great miracles performed. The truth was that Jesus was going to take these seeming insignificant loaves and fishes, step onto the trading floor of Heaven, and feed a multitude. As Jesus took these loaves and fishes and in the spirit stepped onto the trading floors of Heaven, a miracle occurred. Just like He took the natural water and from the trading floors turned it into supernatural wine, He is taking the small amount of the boy's food and trading it into something huge that could meet the needs of tens of thousands. The result was a multiplication from the trading floors of Heaven. The little became much when it was brought to the trading floors in the spirit realm of Heaven.

There were several things involved in Jesus taking this boy's food and multiplying it on the trading floors of Heaven. First, the Bible says Jesus used this whole scenario to "test" the disciples. He was putting them in a situation where they felt awkward and unsure. He was expanding their thinking out of the natural realm and into the spiritual realm. They were going to have to do something that made them uncomfortable. When we step onto the trading floors of Heaven, it is always a test. Are we going to stay in the natural realm or believe God and step into the spiritual dimension? In regard to our finances or any other sacrifice, this always involves a test. Will we take what is secure in our hand—everything from our finances to our very lives—and offer it and potentially move something in the spirit and see a miracle, or hold it in the natural and stay in status quo? The apostle Paul spoke of this in Second Corinthians 8:8. He clearly says to them that they are being tested in regard to the giving of finances.

I speak not by commandment, but I am testing the sincerity of your love by the diligence of others.

It is always a test when we take our finances and use them for something spiritual. We are taking that which seems so natural and using it in the spirit realm. We are taking what is precious to us as an expression of our heart, faith, love, and passion and trading with it for what money can't buy. Second Corinthians 8:4-5 declares we give ourselves first and then our money is an expression of this.

Imploring us with much urgency that we would receive the gift and the fellowship of the ministering to the saints. And not only as we had hoped, but they first gave themselves to the Lord, and then to us by the will of God.

When we give ourselves first to the Lord, our money is used on the trading floors of Heaven as an expression. It manifests in the natural realm our hearts in the spirit realm. Just like Noah offered literal, natural animals on an altar, we by faith take our natural finances and shift things in the spirit as well. We make trades and enter into dimensions of faith, love, and passion that stir the heart of God as it is received before Him.

Another significant thing Jesus did with the loaves and fishes as He stepped onto the trading floors of Heaven was He gave thanks. Giving thanks speaks of worship and worth. By giving thanks, Jesus was declaring He valued what He held in His hand. He wasn't complaining about what He didn't have. He was thankful for what He did have. A thankful heart is powerful on the trading floors of Heaven. When we approach the trading floors of Heaven, a heart of worship and worth is essential. Every offering we bring to the trading floors of Heaven must be laced with a thankful and worshipful spirit. Paul spoke of this in Philippians 4:6. We are told to have our prayers filled with this spirit of thankfulness.

> *Be anxious for nothing, but in everything by prayer and supplication, with thanksgiving, let your requests be made known to God.*

We don't come in bitterness or anger. This is not the way we approach the trading floors of Heaven. We come yielded and in humility and surrender. As we do, our trade will be accepted before the Lord. We can see this contrast in the lives of Mary and Martha at the death of their brother Lazarus. John 11:20-21 shows Martha basically accusing Jesus of not caring and being too late.

> *Now Martha, as soon as she heard that Jesus was coming, went and met Him, but Mary was sitting in the house. Now Martha said to Jesus,*

> *"Lord, if You had been here, my brother would not have died."*

A few verses later in John 11:32 we see Mary coming in a heart of worship saying the same identical words. Her words, however, are filled with worship.

> *Then, when Mary came where Jesus was, and saw Him, she fell down at His feet, saying to Him, "Lord, if You had been here, my brother would not have died."*

We must come on the trading floors with worship and thankfulness. Paul again exhorts men to pray without anger and in holiness.

> *I desire therefore that the men pray everywhere, lifting up holy hands, without wrath and doubting* (1 Timothy 2:8).

Holiness empowers our prayers. The absence of anger speaks of a surrendered, thankful, and worshipful heart as our prayers are offered. May the Lord reach deep into our spirits and heal every wound that would fester into thanklessness. Then we can approach the trading floors of Heaven with a clean heart and a right spirit.

A final thought to functioning on the trading floors of Heaven—in this miracle, the multiplication happened as the substance was passed from hand to hand. Once Jesus had made the trade in the spirit realm, something practical was done. Jesus commanded the elements of food be passed from hand to hand. This is where the multiplication functionally happened. The spiritual unseen force that produced it occurred on a trading floor in Heaven. The actual manifestation of the multiplication occurred as the disciples passed the bread and fishes out. They stepped into the miracle that had been released through the trade of Jesus on the trading floors of Heaven. If we are to see miracles revealed, we must add our natural to the spiritual. We must trade. We also must act from that trade to see miraculous things done. This so often is the downfall of the believer to seeing the miraculous. We are more than willing to do the spiritual but are reluctant to add the natural. As a result, we don't see the supernatural realm released in our lives. Even when Jesus healed people, He would consistently tell them to, "Take up your bed and walk" (John 5:8). They had to add their natural to Jesus' supernatural to get the miracle. What would have happened had the disciples not passed out the bread and fishes? The miracle would not have occurred. Everything would have stayed the same. Nothing would have changed. Even though everything was in place in the spirit realm for the miracle to take place it would have been forfeited. We must be aggressive in our faith. We must not be passive. We must do what is necessary on the trading floors of Heaven but then move from them as well. When we do, great breakthrough can happen.

The trading floors in the spirit realm are very real and powerful. We are called and commissioned to step onto them. From these places, we can trade to see destinies unlocked, miracles obtained, and supernatural dimensions entered. Don't be bashful and allow your uncertainty to hold you back. Position your heart before the Lord and take a step onto the trading floors of Heaven. Great breakthroughs and releases await you.

11

LET'S GET TRADING

IT IS TIME FOR YOU TO START TRADING! THIS IS NOT JUST something to read about and then say, "Well, that was interesting." The trading floors are real, but until you take a step of faith you will never experience them. Let's keep some key principles as you start to trade

WE ARE ROYAL PRIESTS WHO SERVE IN THE TRUE TABERNACLE

We are part of a holy priesthood and Jesus is our High Priest. As Robert explained earlier, when we bring our tithe from a heart of honor and not duty, we connect to this heavenly priesthood. Under the New Covenant, one is not required to bring a tithe, but we can choose to bring the tithe because we want to honor our High Priest. Hebrews 7:8 tells us that under the Old Covenant mortal men received tithes, but now Jesus receives our tithes in Heaven. The act of bringing the tithe is no longer a matter of obedience but a matter of honor. The bringing of the tithe illustrates that the believer understands that Jesus is now seated at the right hand of the Father and is administrating as High Priest. When you bring a tithe in honor of Jesus and His work at the cross, you tithe gives witness that you acknowledge His positon as High Priest. You acknowledge that you are connected to this priesthood that serves at the altar in Heaven and are a part of the New Covenant.

I want to take a moment to be very clear on this. You are not required to tithe to be a part of the New Covenant. There is no curse that will come upon you if you do not tithe and you will not be excluded from the New Covenant or the priesthood. If you choose not to bring a tithe, that is your free choice. If you do choose to tithe, it is not in order to get something or earn something from God. Rather the tithe is freely given because you have *already* been blessed abundantly as a result of being part of the New Covenant. When I think of what it means to have been set free from the law of sin and death and been given abundant, eternal life through Christ Jesus, the Mediator and High Priest of this New Covenant, the only way that I can think to thank and honor Him is to do what Abraham did—bring Him a tithe. The tithe is then offered from a heart of honor and love for the One who showers me with blessings daily. The tithe then is a voluntary response of love and honor of Jesus, my High Priest.

When given from this heart, I believe that the tithe is a freewill offering that releases testimony before the throne, witnessing to our recognition of Jesus, our High Priest who receives our tithes "there" and our acceptance of our role as a priest in His royal priesthood spoken of in First Peter 2:9.

The reality is that under the New Covenant, we are a royal priesthood that operates from the temple in Heaven and it is as a part of this priesthood that we bring our spiritual sacrifices and step onto the trading floors of Heaven.

TRADING RELEASES THE KINGDOM TO US

When we look at trading on God's trading floor, we must bear in mind that His trading floor exists so that He can *release* the Kingdom to us so that it can be established in us and then through us into the world. This trading floor is all about what God can *give* to us. Satan wants to *steal* from us on his trading floor; God is looking to *give* to us.

TRADING IS ABOUT GOD'S DESIRES

Trading is all about the desires of God's heart and not about the desires of our hearts. When we offer ourselves as a living sacrifice, we step onto God's trading floor. Now we are positioned to hear the desires of His heart. This is what Isaiah did in Isaiah 6:8:

> *Also I heard the voice of the Lord, saying: "Whom shall I send, and who will go for Us?" Then I said, "Here am I! Send me."*

God gave access to Isaiah, as a prophet under the Old Covenant, to be in the throne room of God. While there, he heard God talking in counsel. He heard that the desire of God's heart to send someone on Their behalf. Isaiah immediately responded and said, "Here am I, send me." He was not asking God if he could go and be a prophet to the nation because it was something that he wanted. No! He was responding to the desire of God's heart. The moment that Isaiah heard what God's desire was, he volunteered to be the vehicle who would carry God's word to the nation. Trading is not about what we want; it is about what God wants.

NO INSTANT GRATIFICATION

The trades that we make on God's trading floor happen in the realm of the spirit. The word or seed that is released to you by God happens in the realm of the spirit. That word has to be tended and nurtured so that at the appointed time it can become manifested on the earth. There is a set time for that purpose to be presented on earth.

> *To everything there is a season, a time for every purpose under Heaven* (Ecclesiastes 3:1).

Everything that is sent from Heaven comes as a seed in its season and time. Nothing arrives fully formed. It has to be birthed and then grow into maturity. It is the same with the purposes for which you trade in Heaven. Very often, the results of your trade are only seen months or years after the fact.

Satan's trading floor is the exact opposite. The moment we trade, we receive the sin he has offered. The satisfaction is immediate, no waiting! The god of this world has so brainwashed us in his ways that we expect the same results when we trade with God. I cannot tell you how many people have whined to me, "This trading thing does not work. I traded yesterday/last week/last month and absolutely nothing happened. I do not think this works." No, trading works, but it works on God's principles and His time.

TRADING DEMANDS DILIGENCE TO SEE THE FRUIT

When Jesus turned the water into wine, as Robert so brilliantly explained, it was an excellent example of a heavenly trade. I want to highlight some elements of this miracle as they are important for us to grasp as we begin to trade.

First, it is important to note that those who performed the miracle were servants in the house. Remember, it is only those who serve in the house who are able to trade. Jesus was reluctant to do what His mother had asked as He knew that His time had not yet come. Yet, it was the obedience and surrender of the servants that drew Jesus to them. They presented themselves before Him as a living sacrifice.

Jesus then released an instruction to them. They heard what was on His heart and immediately obeyed. They responded to His words with a spiritual sacrifice of faithful service. Not only was the service faithful, but it was also full of faith. The servants went about their task believing that it would produce what Jesus required. They did not second-guess Him. They did not murmur among themselves about what a stupid idea this was. No, they trusted implicitly and worked hard until the job was finished. They used their natural abilities and natural resources to bring a spiritual sacrifice of service. Once they had completed the task. The miracle was done. The water was now wine. But they would never have seen the fruit of their trade if they had not continued to listen for Jesus' voice and obeyed His next command to, "Draw some out now, and take it to the Master of the Feast" (John 2:8). If they had just finished bringing their sacrifice and gone back to what they were doing, the miracle (the fruit of the trade) would have sat unnoticed and no one would have benefitted from it. Many times we do not see the results of our trade and the world does not benefit from them because we do not follow them up diligently.

We see the same principle at work in the multiplication of the bread and the fishes in John 6:5-13. After Jesus had stepped onto the trading floor in Heaven and made His sacrifice of thanksgiving, the bread and the fish held the miraculous potential of the Kingdom. But it was not until the disciples obeyed Jesus' instruction to distribute the food that the miracle was seen and the community benefitted. There is always a practical walking out of a trade in order to see the fruit.

PRACTICAL WAYS TO BEGIN TRADING

It is time for you to take a step of faith and begin to put what you have learned into action. I encourage you, the next time you are planning to go to a worship service, prepare yourself as a living sacrifice before you arrive at the church. Take some time to lay your life down—lay aside your mindsets, your agenda, your way of doing things. Forgive all those you need to forgive. Deal with any frustrations or wrong heart attitudes toward the Lord. You want clean hands and a pure heart as you go to the house of the Lord. Be intentional about becoming that living sacrifice.

Enter into the time of worship with intent to ascend the hill of the Lord, bringing your sacrifice of thanksgiving and praise. When you find yourself before the throne and the heavy weight of His presence is around you, be aware that you are also in front a trading floor. If you are able to see in the realm of the spirit, you may even see coals of fire. If you are struggling with sickness or heaviness of heart, take this opportunity to make a divine exchange. Step onto that trading floor and lay down your illness. Lay down your tiredness and hopelessness. Lay down all that seeks to entangle you, and step into a fresh revelation of Jesus. Receive a new and fresh perspective from Him.

At offering time, do not just do what you have always done! Now you know that your offering is also your sacrifice, which is your worship. You understand the great power of your sacrifice to shift things in the natural realm. You understand that your offering has a voice before the Lord. Do something different! Bring an offering that costs you something. Bring a memorial offering that will cause God to remember you and your house. Be intentional!

As you walk from your seat to the basket, step onto God's trading floor in the realm of the spirit and bring your offering layered on top of your living sacrifice. Check that your heart is in a place of worship and that the testimony of your offering is a good one. Ask the Lord to accept your offerings as a sweet-smelling incense before Him. If you are able, watch in the realm of the spirit to see how the fire begins to burn the sacrifice.

During the time of prophetic words or the preaching, be attentive to the prompting of Holy Spirit. Have an ear to hear the heart desires of God expressed in the meeting. When you hear those Kingdom seeds being released, be a volunteer. Bring your freewill offering so that the seed will find fertile ground. That freewill offering might be a financial offering. It might be an offer to help with a ministry project in the church. It might be a missions trip. It might simply be inviting a widow for dinner. It will be a voluntary spiritual sacrifice that *volunteers* your life as the good soil for the Kingdom seed. Your life becomes the ground where the Kingdom of God can take root, grow up, and bear a harvest in your life.

And this does not only have to be in church. Take time to present yourself as a living sacrifice every morning. Maintain a heart of worship toward the Lord throughout your day. That includes the way in which you do your work. Be faithful in your service to your employer as unto the Lord. This is a spiritual sacrifice. Treat it as such! Keep your spiritual ears open for opportunities to trade with God. You are not simply keeping busy between church services, you are *doing business until He comes*. Your daily life provides countless trading opportunities whereby you can *bring increase through trading*.

You have been made a king and a priest of the Most High God. You have a responsibility to be fruitful, multiply, fill the earth, subdue it, and have dominion. Your ability to bring spiritual sacrifices and trade on the trading floors of Heaven is going to play an essential part in you fulfilling this destiny. Cities and nations are waiting for you to bring offerings in righteousness that will cause God to come near to them and bring deliverance. Don't be bashful or intimidated. Step on the trading floors of Heaven and be amazed at what God will do in you and though you for His name's sake!

12

Prayers to Access the Trading Floors of Heaven

Prayers to Reverse Demonic Trades

A Practical Example of a Trade Made Through Sin and How to Reverse It

As I have said before, every time that we choose to partake of sin, we trade something away. The enemy is always tempting us to sin because he knows that this is how he can take our godly inheritance and life of prosperity from us.

One of the most common types of sin that he always seeks to draw us into is sexual sin. Scripture is clear that this type of sin causes great corruption to our bodies and souls (see 1 Cor. 6:16-18), and this is why the enemy puts a lot of time into tempting us with sexual sin. With this sin, you join yourself to another person physically and in the soul realm. People indulge in sexual sin for a variety of reasons. Some to satisfy fleshly lust, some for a feeling of acceptance or love, some for a sense of domination. The reasons we partake of sin are many and varied, but no matter what your reason—you are choosing to trade a part of yourself to the enemy, both physically and spiritually, in order to receive what you want. This is what makes this trade so deadly—it gives the enemy direct access to your physical body and your soul.

The enemy takes the access you have traded to him and establishes a demonic gateway into your life. The enemy can then use this gate to send physical tormentors against you in the way of sickness and disease as well as soulish tormenting spirits against you. These spirits will rob you of your self-worth, your identity in Christ, and anything else they can take from you. Remember that when sin is full grown it leads to death (see James 1:15).

In order to reverse this trade, one needs to understand and acknowledge the sin before God. There needs to be a heartfelt confession and repentance. Remember that repentance is not simply words we say but is a determination to turn away from sin and pursue righteousness. The blood of Jesus and the work of the cross needs to be appropriated through this repentance.

Once the sin has been dealt with, we can bring a claim in the courts of Heaven for a full dismantling of the gate, a revoking of all access, and a return of everything that was taken during the trade. Once we have appropriated this through the courts, we go to the trading floor of Heaven. Here we lay down everything that we received in the trade, which includes all the misery, shame, pain, and whatever else has come through that demonic gate. We give it to the Father, and then through the blood of Jesus we receive forgiveness. We receive back all that has been lost. We experience a restoration at the trading floor.

Reversing Trades Made Through Sexual Sin

> *Father, I come to present myself before Your throne of grace. According to Hebrews 4:16, we can boldly come to You in this place in order to obtain mercy and find grace to help in time of need.*
>
> *Father, I come to You today because I have sinned. I come to confess my sin to You and to plead for Your mercy. I confess that I have committed fornication (or any other sexual sin). I acknowledge that I stepped onto satan's trading floor and agreed to partake of the sin of fornication. I realize that I did this with a heart of rebellion toward You and I confess this also as sin. I repent of my actions and my heart attitude. I repent that I chose to worship satan in that moment and I chose to turn my back on You. Please forgive me and have mercy on me.*

Father, I repent. I am so sorry. I turn away from immorality and rebellion. I ask that You would forgive me of this sin. I want to walk in Your paths of righteousness with a heart that loves and honors You.

Father, I ask that the blood of Jesus would speak for me regarding this sin in the court of Heaven. I ask that the sound of the blood and the full work of Jesus on the cross, in which He paid the price for this sin, would now be applied to my sin. The Scripture says in First John 1:9 that if we confess our sin, You are faithful and just to forgive us and to cleanse us from all unrighteousness. Father, I come today to stand on this Word. As I have confessed and repented, I thank You that I am forgiven. I thank You also that the blood of Jesus washes this sin away, removing it as far as the east is from the west according to Psalms 103:12.

And I thank You that the blood of Jesus also cleanses me from this unrighteousness. Every place where my body or soul was defiled through this sin, I ask that the blood of Jesus would cleanse me from this defilement. I ask that the demonic gateway that was established in my body and soul would now be uprooted, overthrown, and removed from me. I ask that the blood would wash over my body, soul, and spirit, removing any defilement or seeds planted in me from partaking of sin. I ask that any sin that has taken root in me through this sin of fornication would now be uprooted completely and burned in the fire of God. I do not want any trace of this sin in my life any longer.

Father, I thank You that because of Your forgiveness and the power of the blood to cleanse me, the enemy no longer has the right to hold my sexual purity from me. Right now I lay a claim before the courts of Heaven for my sexual purity to be returned to me as the enemy no longer has a legal right to hold it. Furthermore, I ask that anything else of my destiny that he is holding based on this sin be given back to me now in the name of Jesus. This trade has been nullified through the blood of Jesus, and I claim back all that was lost in this trade in Jesus' name. I ask that everything that was lost be placed back into the hands of Jesus so that He can cleanse it and release it back to me in His time.

Father, I now choose to step onto Your trading floor and trade all the shame, sorrow, pain, and heartache that I carry because of this trade. I lay down all my feelings of rejection and unworthiness that came with this trade. I believe that I have been forgiven and cleansed, and I will no longer hold on to the fruit of this trade with the enemy. I choose to willingly lay it down on Your altar. I give back everything that I received from this trade with the enemy. I do not want it. I only want my inheritance through Jesus Christ. On Your trading floor,

> *I now receive forgiveness. I receive Your love and acceptance. I receive a fresh sexual purity. And now I choose to worship You and lay myself down as a living sacrifice on Your altar. May my life be a sweet-smelling incense before You.*

A Practical Example of a Curse Operating Because of a Demonic Trade

Robert explains in his book *Unlocking Destinies from the Courts of Heaven* that one of the traits of a curse operating in your life is "lack of prosperity and diminished returns from your labors." If you are working hard and being diligent with your finances yet never seem to walk in the prosperity that Scripture speaks about, you are more than likely laboring under a curse. Invariably, these types of curses have come to you as a generational inheritance because of covenants and contracts that your ancestors made with demonic gods.

When one is experiencing continued financial lack and failure to thrive, it is highly likely that the enemy is laying claim to your finances because of a trade that was made by someone in your bloodline. As I explained in an earlier chapter, in ancient times trades were regularly made with demonic gods in order to secure favor from them. One of the main gods who promised prosperity was Baal. Many cultures brought sacrifices to the god Baal in order to trade for prosperity. In some cultures, they sacrificed to Baal in order to get rain. In other cultures, they sacrificed to Baal to gain strength over their enemies so that they could capture cities and territories, thereby increasing their wealth and influence. The bottom line is that many of our ancestors entered into covenants with this god in order to prosper. Let's take a closer look at what those trades looked like.

A person would come to the altar of the god Baal with their offering. The greater the trade they wanted to make, the greater their offering. It was very common for people to offer their children to Baal in return for prosperity. They stepped onto the trading floor and agreed that Baal could lay claim to all the wealth of their future generations if he would give them prosperity or wealth now. They would then offer the child as a sacrifice and a first fruit of the generations to come. The blood of the sacrifice would ratify the covenant. It also set the rest of the generations apart and dedicated them to Baal. This covenant may have been repeated in successive generations, strengthening it.

Based on this covenant, Baal now has a legal right to draw on you and your wealth because it has been promised to him. He will never take everything from you all at once. He will allow you to have just enough to live on and get by, because he wants to ensure that he can siphon everything that God has assigned to you out of your life. When I see someone in this situation, I always see how the enemy has set up a huge funnel over their life. Every time God releases an opportunity or wealth for a certain purpose, it gets funneled away before it ever reaches the person. They are laboring faithfully, doing everything they know to do, but never seem to experience the abundance that God promises. Why? Because their ancestors have already traded it away.

Prayers to Reverse Trades that Cause Curses

> Father, today I come to You on behalf of my bloodline on both my mother's and father's side—all the way back to Adam. I want to repent on behalf of the ancestor who willingly entered into a covenant with Baal. I repent that we did not know You or trust You to provide for us. I repent that out of our fear we chose to serve another god. We chose to bring our sacrifice to another god in order to secure our futures. I repent of this sin. The Scripture says that we shall have no other gods before You, and in my bloodline we have served other gods. I ask You to please forgive me.
>
> I repent that we did not care about or value our future generations but willingly gave them up in order to secure our own lives. Father, please forgive our selfishness and self-seeking pride. I repent for the sacrifices that we brought to the god Baal. I repent for the offering of human and animal sacrifices as worship on the altar of Baal. I repent for the shedding of innocent blood in sacrifice in order to ratify a covenant with Baal. Please forgive me for this grievous sin in our bloodline. I take responsibility for this sin and I ask You to please forgive us. Father, I ask that as I confess my sin to You and turn from the wicked ways of my ancestors You would forgive me and cleanse me from this unrighteousness.

Father, today I say that I have chosen to serve Jesus Christ. I will have no other gods beside You. As for me and my house, we have chosen to serve the Living God. We declare that You are our only Provider and Deliverer. I ask that the blood of Jesus would speak on my behalf in the courts of Heaven and would wash away these sins that are being used against me as a legal right to steal the blessing of God from my life. I ask that the covenant with Baal that was made by my forefathers would now be annulled in the courts of Heaven. I ask, according to Colossians 2:14, that this handwriting of ordinance that is standing against me would be nailed to the cross with all its legal requirements.

I thank You that the work of Christ at the cross dealt with this covenant 2,000 years ago, and I am appropriating that victory today in the courts. I ask that, as this covenant is annulled, the legal right to continue to divert the generational blessing apportioned to my family would be removed in the name of Jesus. I ask that all the strategies and plans of the enemy to steal our blessings—financial, spiritual, and physical—would now be cancelled and dismantled in the name of Jesus. I ask that the blood of Jesus would redeem everything lost through this trade with the enemy. I now ask that everything that has been lost to my generations through this trade would be recovered and placed back into the hands of Jesus.

Father, I step onto Your trading floor, and I lay down everything that I may have received through this covenant with Baal. I give back any advantage that my generations have enjoyed because of this covenant. I give back all power, influence, wealth, thinking, or any other thing we received—in the natural or in the spirit realm—I do not want it. I only want my inheritance that Jesus died to win for me. Today, I come to acknowledge You as my Source. I lay down all my fears about finances and the future. I lay down all my striving and labors. I lay down all my doubts about You. I trade these for a fresh revelation of Jehovah Jireh, my Provider. I thank You that today You are giving me a new vision as I stand on Your trading floor. I thank You that You have given me the power to get wealth that You may establish Your covenant (see Deut. 8:18). I receive it today. I receive a fresh impartation of Your entrepreneurial spirit. I receive new ideas and opportunities. I honor the generations that went before me. Give me eyes to see the redemptive purposes that lie dormant in my bloodline. By faith I stir them up again today that we would walk in the fullness of the blessings that have been written for me and my house.

A Practical Example of Sickness Operating as a Result of a Demonic Trade

In an earlier chapter, I talked about how we can step onto the trading floor of Heaven to exchange our sickness for healing. I call this a divine exchange. Scripture clearly says that by His stripes we are healed, which means that divine health is something that was won for us at the cross. But we do not always walk in this victory.

I believe this is because we need to discern the cause of the sickness. Sometimes, we simply have a sickness due to the rigors of life. Many times we become ill because we fail to care for our physical bodies as we should. We eat incorrectly, fail to exercise, or generally steward our bodies improperly. This often results in sickness. These types of sicknesses require us to step onto the trading floors and repent for abusing our bodies. We need to repent for not taking care of this dimension of our life. It requires repentance and a real changing of our ways. As we acknowledge our sin and change our ways, we can lay down these sicknesses and experience the healing that Jesus won for us at the cross.

Sickness can also be a manifestation of a sickness in our soul. When we step onto the trading floors of Heaven to lay down our sickness, very often this exposes the wound in our soul that needs to be healed. Once that wounding is dealt with, the sickness leaves our body and we experience divine healing.

But there are also sicknesses that operate as a result of demonic trades. I have seen that many times when people enter into trades with demonic gods in order to gain power over others they suffer from sickness as a result of that trade. I have seen the best examples of this when dealing with generational trades for power. For example, where families have ancestors who were involved in Freemasonry or other secret societies, we often see sicknesses involving respiratory problems and lung diseases. Once the person repents of entering into covenants with these organizations and the gods behind them, the sickness leaves their body. This is just one example, but there are often legal rights that allow the enemy to inflict a person with sickness. These legal rights need to be identified, repented of, and then the healing can be released at God's trading floor.

Prayer to Reverse Sickness and Disease

> *Father God, we humbly come before Your throne of grace today. We find ourselves in a time of need and You say that we can come boldly to You to find grace to help in these times. Father, I have a sickness in my body and I know that it does not come from You. I also know that at the cross, Jesus' blood was shed so that I could be healed. I know and believe this to be true, but I still experience the symptoms of my disease.*
>
> *Father, I want to be free from this sickness. I want to healed and whole. So I step onto Your trading floor before Your throne and I lay down my sickness. I lay each symptom at Your feet. I no longer want to carry it. I choose to exchange it for Your divine health and healing.*

As you lay each symptom at His feet, you will sense in your spirit if you are able to lay them down or not. If you cannot lay them down—and they seem to stick to you—then let's continue praying.

> *Father, I want to lay this down, but for some reason it seems to be a part of me. I ask You to show me where I have given permission for this sickness to be a part of me. I choose to lay aside the physical symptoms of this illness so that You can show me the root cause. Father, I declare today that I want to be healed. I will deal with anything that You show me and repent of anything that I need to repent of, but I want to be free of this sickness.*
>
> *I know that the blood of Jesus is powerful enough to heal and deliver me from any and every disease.*

Begin to lay down each symptom again, and when one gets stuck ask the Father to reveal the root cause to you. It may be an emotional wounding, in which case you may need to forgive some people or allow Holy Spirit to minister to you on an issue. It may also be that the Lord shows you a legal right in your bloodline. If that is the case, then you need to repent of the iniquity and deal with any covenants or contracts in the court before stepping back onto the trading floor of Heaven and continuing to pray.

> *Father, I thank You that You have revealed these root causes to me. I thank You for the blood of Jesus, which has already won the victory for me. Thank You that today I can lay down my sickness on Your*

> *altar, and because of the blood of Jesus I can receive forgiveness and divine healing. I thank You that His blood is speaking for me today. I receive the words of life that are being spoken by the blood of Jesus. I receive healing from the Father in every part of my body, soul, and spirit that was afflicted. In Jesus' name.*

PRAYERS TO TRADE ON GOD'S TRADING FLOOR

The key to trading on the trading floor of Heaven is to be intentional in bringing your sacrifices. And I am not only talking about finances. There are many types of sacrifices that we can bring to the Lord, and we should always be looking for how we can bring those freewill offerings. Here are some examples to get you started.

Faithful Service

This is a type of sacrifice that you can bring to the Lord that can be a sweet-smelling aroma. Your work is your worship. Be intentional about offering it as a sacrifice.

> *Father, today I come to You at the beginning of my day. I have offered myself as a living sacrifice on Your altar. I want my life to be a sweet-smelling aroma to You today. I choose to stay on Your trading floor, and I present my work before You today. (You can bring a specific project if you wish or a specific service you are doing for the Lord.)*

Father, You are the One who has empowered me to do this work. You have given me the resources I need to be able to do it, and so I go out today with a happy heart—grateful and privileged that I can serve You in my place of business. I give You my hours of work today as a sacrifice. I choose to work diligently and faithfully so that Your name will be glorified in all that I do.

I pray that as I bring this sacrifice, You will accept it and that it will be a sweet-smelling aroma to You. I trust that as this aroma ascends into Heaven, You will remember me and my workplace and You will bless every person there. Father, You have blessed me; now let me be a blessing to all those in my workplace so that Your name would be lifted up among all the people.

Voluntary Offerings

Remember how I said that when God releases a word to us we can volunteer to be a part of what He is doing by bringing our freewill offering? Well, that does not only apply in the church. Nor does it only apply to financial offerings. As you go through life, keep your ear tuned to the Holy Spirit. You may hear Him ask you to pay for lunch for a colleague. He may prompt you to talk to someone whom you have not spoken with before in the office. He may ask you to pray for someone in the bathroom who is crying. God is always moving—it is up to us to position ourselves to work with Him. And when you do hear God, respond! And present it as a voluntary offering.

For example, you felt the Holy Spirit prompt you to offer to buy lunch for your colleague. God is wanting to intervene in that person's life. He needs someone to partner with Him. You can be that person. This is your opportunity to trade with God.

> *Father, thank You that You are giving me the opportunity to co-labor with You. Thank You that I can sow into what You are doing in X's life. I step onto Your trading floor, and I present my sacrifice of time and money as a freewill offering. I pray that it rises to You as a sweet-smelling aroma. I ask that as I bring this sacrifice, You will intervene in X's life and bring her into a place of peace with You.*

The Sacrifice of Praise

Never believe the lie that you have nothing to bring to the Lord! We all have a voice, and we can use it to bring praises to God. "Therefore by Him let us continually offer the sacrifice of praise to God, that is the fruit of our lips, giving thanks to His name" (Heb. 13:15).

> *Father, today I step onto Your trading floor before Your throne. I thank You for the sacrifice of Jesus that made it possible for me to stand here. And as I stand before You, I lay down all the heavy weights that seek to entangle me. I lay down the false burdens that I have picked up. I lay down the spirit of heaviness, and I receive the garment of praise.*

I thank You that I am alive and I have a destiny and a calling in You. I am fearfully and wonderfully made, and You watch over me day and night. You are my strong tower, my Provider, the One who delivers me from all my enemies. When all my friends desert me, You never leave me or forsake me. Thank You, Jesus! I sing Your praise! There is no one like You!

As you trade your worries and concerns and burdens, you start to praise Him. He will lift you out of every place of misery, despair, or mediocrity. When we lay down our stuff, He can release His life to us!

What are you waiting for? Let's start trading!

About Beverley Watkins

Beverley Watkins is a recognized seer prophet and apostolic voice with specialized, practical knowledge on legislating in the courts of Heaven.

She is an author and international speaker, activating and equipping believers in their roles as kings and priests of God. She also works closely with leaders to develop strategies for reforming the seven mountains of culture in order to see nations fulfill their destiny.

Beverley and her husband, Robin, are based in Johannesburg, South Africa, where they lead Global Impact—a non profit company that equips the Ekklesia for the reformation of nations. They are apostolically aligned with Robert Henderson and Global Reformers.

About Robert Henderson

Robert Henderson is a global apostolic leader who operates in revelation and impartation. His teaching empowers the Body of Christ to see the hidden truths of Scripture clearly and apply them for breakthrough results. Driven by a mandate to disciple nations through writing and speaking, Robert travels extensively around the globe, teaching on the apostolic, the Kingdom of God, and most notably, the Courts of Heaven. He has been married to Mary for 40 years. They have six children and five grandchildren. Together they are enjoying life in beautiful Midlothian, TX.

INCREASE THE EFFECTIVENESS OF YOUR PRAYERS.

Learn how to release your destiny from Heaven's Courts!

Unlocking Destinies from the Courts of Heaven
Curriculum Box Set Includes:
9 Video Teaching Sessions (2 DVD Disks), Unlocking Destinies *book, Interactive Manual, Leader's Guide*

There are books in Heaven that record your destiny and purpose. Their pages describe the very reason you were placed on the Earth.

And yet, there is a war against your destiny being fulfilled. Your archenemy, the devil, knows that as you occupy your divine assignment, by default, the powers of darkness are demolished. Heaven comes to Earth as God's people fulfill their Kingdom callings!

In the *Unlocking Destinies from the Courts of Heaven* book and curriculum, Robert Henderson takes you step by step through a prophetic prayer strategy. By watching the powerful video sessions and going through the Courts of Heaven process using the interactive manual, you will learn how to dissolve the delays and hindrances to your destiny being fulfilled.

Experience a personal revival!

Spirit-empowered content from today's top Christian authors delivered directly to your inbox.

Join today!
lovetoreadclub.com

Inspiring Articles
Powerful Video Teaching
Resources for Revival

Get all of this and so much more, e-mailed to you twice weekly!

LOVE TO READ CLUB
by **D** DESTINY IMAGE